# Pet Prayers
# & Blessings

# Pet Prayers
# & Blessings

Ceremonies & Celebrations to Share
with the Animals You Love

Laurie Sue Brockway & Victor Fuhrman

STERLING

New York / London

Special prayer permissions may be found on page 191.

STERLING and the distinctive Sterling logo are
registered trademarks of Sterling Publishing Co., Inc.

Published by Sterling Publishing Co., Inc.
387 Park Avenue South, New York, NY 10016
© 2008 by Laurie Sue Brockway and Victor Fuhrman
Distributed in Canada by Sterling Publishing
c/o Canadian Manda Group, 165 Dufferin Street
Toronto, Ontario, Canada M6K 3H6
Distributed in the United Kingdom by GMC Distribution Services
Castle Place, 166 High Street, Lewes, East Sussex, England BN7 1XU
Distributed in Australia by Capricorn Link (Australia) Pty. Ltd.
P.O. Box 704, Windsor, NSW 2756, Australia

Design and Layout: Scott Meola, Simplissimus

ISBN 978-1-4027-4152-4

# DEDICATION

*To our children,*

Abby, Alexander, and Kismet

*For the furry babies we have loved:*

Kabbalah and Kitov

Jezzabelle

Scooter

Foxie Lady

Pookie

Muffin

Pi and Sandy

Boo and Grace

Frances and Snowy

Susie

Sherry

Phoenix

and Topazia

# Native American Prayer

*Oh Great Spirit! I give you thanks for creating all of the peoples;*
*Two legged, four legged, winged and finned.*
*May I learn the great lessons from each of these . . .*
*From the Cat, let me learn healing, clarity, and keen vision.*
*From the Bird, let me learn how to let my spirit soar.*
*From the Fish, let me learn tenacity and to overcome obstacles.*
*From the Horse, let me learn strength and freedom.*
*And from the Dog, let me learn faithfulness, courage,*
*and unconditional love.*
*May I walk, swim, and fly in harmony*
*and balance with all of these. Aho!*

—VICTOR FUHRMAN

# ACKNOWLEDGMENTS

We are so grateful to the many pet lovers who helped make this book a reality.

First, we thank the dozens who shared their insights and experiences with us in interviews and questionnaires, and the special group of people who offered "Pet Tales" for the book, including Reverend Sandra Lee Schubert, Gay Hendricks, Holly Fairchild, Carole Mumford, Diane Brackett, and Mike Diamond.

We also thank our friend Father Paul Keenan, as well as Loree Mason O'Neill and The Pet Prayer Line for allowing us to use their prayers.

A special expression of gratitude to our colleague Marty Tousley, of SelfHealingExpressions.com, for sharing her wisdom.

Big thanks to our agents Arielle Ford and Brian Hilliard, and our editors Patty Gift and Anne Barthel.

Our training as interfaith ministers taught us how to create rituals and prayers and how to bless all sentient beings. We are thankful to our first training ground, The New Seminary in New York. Most of all, we were blessed to have studied with Rabbi Joseph Gelberman, pioneer of the concept of interfaith ministry. Without him, our work in this field would not have been possible.

# CONTENTS

# PREFACE

In the fall of 2005, we decided to fulfill our son Alexander's wish for a dog. He had always demonstrated a tremendous love for animals and an ability to communicate with them in subtle and joyous ways. So when he began to campaign in earnest for an animal companion, we felt it would be good for him to have a new furry best friend.

We visited several local shelters and were touched and saddened by the number of dogs that had been abandoned or given up for adoption because their owners could no longer care for them. After several weeks of visits, we decided that it was time to take Alex with us.

As "responsible" adults and parents, we explained to him that he would see many wonderful animals that day and would probably want to adopt all of them. We asked him not to get upset if we didn't find the "right" dog on this first outing. As he had turned fourteen the month before, we felt he was mature enough to handle this.

We visited several shelters and experienced the requisite number of "ooohs" and "ahhhs" and "awws," but the magical connection did not occur. We each had our own idea of what the "ideal" pet would be. Laurie Sue, for example, was adamant that we had to have a small dog. "Big enough to tumble around with Alexander, but small enough to fit in a carrying case. About fourteen pounds is my max."

We arrived at The Little Shelter in Northport, New York, at around 3:30 P.M. I dropped off Laurie Sue and Alex and went to park the car. When I arrived at the shelter office, I saw Laurie Sue sitting on the side with a strange, resigned smile on her face and her finger pointing to the floor. There, in the middle of the office floor, sat a laughing and excited Alexander with a dog almost as big as he, climbing all over him and licking his face like it was candy.

This excited chocolate, coffee, and white-coated dog with one blue eye and one brown-gold eye—named Katrina because she had been rescued as a pup from Hurricane Katrina—was being returned by a couple who had adopted her a month before. They already had a dog at home and it did not get along with Katrina. They had been returning her at the same moment that Alex and Laurie Sue walked in. Katrina saw Alex and immediately ran to play with him.

One of the shelter workers asked if Alex would like to play with Katrina in a private pen, and we agreed. The play was natural and happy, and they looked more like reunited friends than boy and dog. Alex turned to us with wide eyes and asked, "Can we keep her?"

We both had doubts and reservations. Laurie Sue hadn't

lived with a canine since she was Alex's age, and it had been a couple of decades since I was a doggie dad. Each of us had had cats in between, and we were more used to pets that sort of took care of themselves. We had just completed our new home together and struggled with the idea of training a forty-pound puppy, especially one that would soon be sixty pounds! We worried about whether Alex could handle her as she got bigger; we were concerned about her reported inability to behave with other dogs. And we knew she had abandonment issues because she had been rescued from the chaos of Katrina.

We ran through all the worries that accompany making a commitment of this kind. Then Alex suggested we have a "bug-hug." This family tradition is borrowed from the old expression "snug as a bug in a rug": whenever we have moments of doubt, fear, or sadness, together or individually, we join in a three-way hug, comforting each other and silently praying for healing, understanding, and peace. Collectively, we said "bug-hug!" and, without prompting, Katrina came over, snuggled into our center, and joined us. In that moment, we knew she was part of our family.

We also knew that Katrina was not the right name for her. The shelter had originally named her Truffles because of her coloring, but that name did not resonate, either. I suggested we name her Kismet, partly because it was serendipity and the divine plan that brought us to the shelter just as she was being returned, and also because she and Alex kissed when they met . . . "kiss-met" . . . Kismet!

We have learned many lessons since we adopted Kismet, about our own strengths and weaknesses; about patience, tests of faith, and tests of our love and unity. It is not always easy bringing a new being into your home. There is a lot of "cross-cultural" communication to be learned. Laurie Sue says she never prayed as much as she did in those first four months of adjusting to being a new dog mommy.

In sending us this marvelous companion, God once again gave us an opportunity to grow and learn and love together, which strengthened us as a family.

It is our hope that this book will open a new level of understanding between you and your pet companion, enrich your life with joy, and deepen your gratitude for the gift of animal stewardship.

In peace,
Reverend Victor Fuhrman

# Pet Prayers & Blessings

# INTRODUCTION

*"Our cats are our masters and I say that about
10 percent facetiously. We have told them that their
function is to reduce stress, yet they do that when they
please. We have no children so they are certainly members
of our family. I am continuously glad I decided not to
have children, as I wouldn't want to spoil a human
being the way we spoil these cats."*

—JANE AND DALE, PROUD PARENTS OF TWO
(OBVIOUSLY) ADORED FELINES

We love our pets. And statistics show that we are willing to
spend oodles on our poodles, kitties, horses, and other animals, keeping them well groomed, stylishly attired, fed,
happy, healthy, and safe.

Americans share their homes with more than 70 million
cats, 60 million dogs, and 2 million or so domestic birds. At
least 65 percent of all homes in the United States include at
least one pet.

"For many of us, pets are as much a part of the family as
any human member," says Dan Neuharth, Ph.D., marriage

and family therapist, and author of *Secrets You Keep from Yourself: How to Stop Sabotaging Your Happiness*.

"Have you ever noticed how, when families go places with their dogs, family members tend to get along better?" he points out. "The humans seem more relaxed, curious, and open. Those who have a dog or pet in tow (or with a pet towing them, as the case may be) seem by and large even-keeled, calmer, and friendlier, and tend to treat each other better than many families without a pet."

Why? "Perhaps it's the unconditional love pets provide. Perhaps having a smaller critter to care for and watch over brings out the best in us. Perhaps pets are so themselves, so congruous, so present, that it gives us humans an inspiring example."

Perhaps pets put us deeply in touch with a state of being that sages and spiritual leaders have tried to help us attain: living in the moment. That's what pets do best! And many would say that "in the moment" is where spirit can be most easily accessed.

Although certain faiths are known for honoring animals and blessing pets, many pet lovers are exploring their spiritual connections to their pets outside the domain of traditional religion, seeking a more nondenominational, multifaith, and even metaphysical approach.

That's where *Pet Prayers & Blessings* comes in.

*Pet Prayers & Blessings* shows how to spiritually include our furry, feathered, or amphibian family members—how to bless them, pray for them, and celebrate with them! It is designed to bring the sacred to daily living and make us even more aware of the preciousness of our everyday rituals with our pets.

As ministers, we are often called upon to provide prayer and healing ceremonies for animals, and we see time and again how meaningful it is for people to include their pets in spiritual services. *Pet Prayers & Blessings* is a unique collection of prayers, blessings, ceremonies, healing rituals, and special celebrations specifically written to address the spiritual needs of pet owners and their beloved pets. Most are original, but we have adapted some classics as well. We offer guidance for pet owners, showing them how to lead prayers, blessings, and ceremonies for pets, along with tips on how to include pets in spiritual events that are led by a clergyperson (such as weddings). We also include stories from pet lovers who share ways they have blessed and been blessed by their companion animals.

We wanted this book to be for *everyone*, so the tone is spiritual, nondenominational, and nonreligious; yet we also honor many different faiths and ways of calling to Divine Presence. You will find elements from different cultures and traditions, such as a Kabbalistic naming ceremony, a Native

American blessing of the elements, and a Celtic prayer to connect with the soul of your animal.

The book also contains:

- Special healing prayers and blessings for animals that are ill, with tips on creating a prayer circle and asking others to help.
- Everyday prayers such as evening prayers, blessings over food, and prayers for pets left alone in the house during the day.
- Ceremonies for special occasions, such as bringing a new pet into the home; blessing a new litterbox, bird cage, or fish tank; and naming and blessing a new baby pet.
- Prayers for the pet owner and family, whether they want to heal allergies, trust that the dog will stop destroying furniture, or ask for blessings for long life with this special companion.
- Memorial prayers, memorial services, and support for grieving.

We hope this book helps to add a new dimension of spirit to your life with your beloved pet!

Many blessings,
Rev. Laurie Sue Brockway

# Part One

## A Multifaith Approach to Prayers for Pets

"I believe that companion animals are God's special gift to us. They are very important, spiritual beings who have much to teach us about life and living in the moment, and about death and dying with acceptance, dignity, and grace. With their constant presence, availability, and devotion, they are our best source of unconditional love, becoming for many of us the ideal child, mate, or friend. They listen without judgment or reproach, and never give advice. They accept us exactly as we are, regardless of how we look or feel or behave. They forgive us readily and never hold grudges against us. No matter how much change we must endure in our unpredictable lives, our animal companions are always there for us."

—MARTY TOUSLEY, GRIEF COUNSELOR AND AUTHOR,
SELFHEALINGEXPRESSIONS.COM

# Chapter One

*Taking a Spiritual Journey with Our Pets*

*"Adorable presence! Thou who art within and without.
Above and below and all around . . . "*

—SWAMI OMKAR, FROM THE PEACE PRAYER

Although most of the world's religions have scriptures and
doctrines related to the care of animals, not all include *specific*
pet prayers, blessings, and rituals you can do with, and for,
your companion animals. However, there are many rich traditions from which we can cull and create pet prayers.

As interfaith ministers we are often called upon to offici-
ate or provide blessings, prayers, healing, and rituals for
pets, and we always treat the situation as if it were a human
occasion. We either adapt existing religious rites, or craft an
appropriate service. For pet funerals and memorials, we celebrate the pet's life, offer prayers of easy transition to the
other side of the "Rainbow Bridge," and honor the loss and

grief the pet's owners are going through. We find that the same sentiments apply, whether the loved one is born of the human race or another part of the animal kingdom.

It is true across the board. Whether a wedding or a memorial, a welcome for a new kitten, or a prayer for an animal that is ill, we've discovered that people find it very meaningful to bless their pets and to have access to the same kind of spiritual services available to humans. They also seem quite relieved to know there are clergy and other people of spirit who look upon furry, feathered, or scaled members of the family with the same respect offered to the folks without wings, fur, or fins.

# A Boom in Honoring Animal Spirituality

In recent years there has been much interest in animal spirituality, and human spiritual connection to animals. We've seen a growing number of books on communicating with animals and exploring pets as our angels and guardians here on earth. We have also seen a huge increase in "Blessings of the Animals" taking place around the country. Once the domain of the Catholic Church and some other Christian denominations, these blessings for all the neighborhood pets are being offered by more and more interfaith and nondenominational groups. Our Pet Prayers and Blessings interfaith ministry offers special blessings as well.

But are our pets actually religious? Can they actively practice a faith? Do *they* pray?

Some pet owners say their animals do, in their own way. Perhaps they are tuning into our energy of peace and silence, or being calmed by the sound of a chant or a blessing offered with a soft voice. Maybe they just love to be with us and seem to organically participate in whatever ritual or celebration we decide to do.

Or perhaps our pups, kitties, birds, and fish are soulful beings that actually groove on the energy of prayer, blessing, ritual, and sacred celebration. Many of the pet people we interviewed while researching this book seem to believe so.

## How Spiritual Is Your Pet?

For example, some animals may naturally seem calm and gentle, even Buddha-like. (We even came across a dog named Buddha.) Others may have a natural disposition that makes them fun companions for a busy summer solstice circle, like the pup we danced and pranced with during a ritual in Central Park. Others might be suited to spiritual visits to a house of worship. We saw a Yorkie in synagogue during the High Holy Days, and the rabbi didn't notice it there, even when a tiny bark emanated from its owner's shoulder bag. The dog was with its whole family. They told us that they just wouldn't think of leaving it behind.

And it's not just dogs who participate in the spiritual life with us, although they are the most likely to be traveling about and participating in family activities. Regardless of the kind of pet you have, if you happen to be a spiritual person, you might find that you have a spiritual pet. Or you might simply find that you look at your animal through spiritual eyes and naturally include him or her in your daily practice.

Perhaps our pets just assume the faith background or spiritual practice of their owners. We've heard of Yoga cats, dogs who do Buddhist meditations, and Wiccan familiars who take part in rituals, and we have seen dogs wearing yarmulkes or crosses. Then again, they themselves come from such diverse breeds and backgrounds that they are multicultural in their own right. Animals are, in the purest sense, universal beings.

So, it seems unfair to label our animals "religious," per se. More likely we think of them as having spirit and soul! Many of us also believe there was a force in the universe—some sort of divine plan, a deity, or an energy—that brought our particular pet into our lives.

Even the nonreligious person can find a way to bless an animal and connect with it spiritually. A prayer or blessing carries a vibration meant to uplift, heal, and make whole again. You can pray in many forms, without ever directing your prayers to any one (any deity or holy name) in particular.

Then again, even people who are not practicing the religion of their birth sometimes find solace in their faith of origin when they need a prayer for a beloved pet. It is completely up to you how you choose to pray with or for your pets, and if you want to include specific religious references at all.

Our colleague Marty Tousley, an amazing pet grief counselor, shared a story about a woman who lost her dog and felt that she needed a ritual from her Jewish faith to help heal her family's pain. She described her family's touching ceremony of remembrance following the death. "As she and her children lit their Sabbath candles that April evening, they included a memorial prayer written by their rabbi, and lit a memorial candle for their dog," Marty shared. "She said they all felt comforted by the religious ritual, finding support and meaning in the words they had not yet been able to express to one another. I was so impressed by this mother's willingness to openly acknowledge and express her family's grief, to include her children in the process, and to turn to her religious tradition for the comfort it provided all of them."

Lori Scott Fogleman, a public relations professional and animal lover, points out how important it is for people to be able to turn *somewhere* for prayer, blessings, and compassion for their animals.

"In my Sunday School class, we've had families, with some trepidation, bring up a health situation with a pet as a prayer request," she says. "It is fear of being laughed at or requesting prayer for something that some might see as insignificant. Yet once they speak the request, they are *so* relieved because everyone responds immediately with such compassion. It isn't 'silly' at all to seek divine guidance for all of God's creatures!"

With that in mind, let's look at the ways different faith traditions view animals and pets, and also at the very personal ways in which pet lovers pray for and honor the spirit of their pets.

# Chapter Two

*Pet Prayers for All Faiths*

Throughout this book, you'll find sentiments and prayers adapted from many of the world's traditions, giving you a wide variety of materials to choose and use as needed. Following is a brief overview of how specific faiths look upon our relationship and responsibility to animals. Out of respect for the traditions that honor the Goddess, or multiple Gods and Goddesses, this book uses an uppercase "G" when referring to these deities.

# Buddhism

*"My belief system regarding animals is that they are living,
feeling creatures, with powers and abilities that we are
usually not aware of and can almost never understand.
I have found dogs to be very healing presences, and cats are
very good at getting secrets out of you!"*

—MIKE DIAMOND

**SACRED TEXT(S):** *Sutras*

**BELIEF ABOUT ANIMALS:** *Animals are divine, evolving beings
and part of the one eternal creation.*

**PRACTICE AND RITUAL:** *Respect for all animals, worship of
animal "devas" such as Garuda (half bird, half human),
elephants, horses, and lions.*

In the Buddhist tradition, prayer is a state of being that
arises out of silence and meditation. There is also chanting
and the evocation of the Jewel in the Lotus for the healing
and protection of all things and all beings (*Om Mani Padme
Hum*). Buddhists put all life on equal footing. For example,
in Tibet, when they built temples, they would try to build
around the worms.

"Buddhism considers all of life to be evolving toward higher
consciousness," says animal communication consultant Sharon

Callahan. "Buddhism considers nonhuman life to be just as divine as human life. Animals are seen to be an evolving kingdom of living creatures destined in time to attain perfect enlightenment. All of life is seen to be one. According to this conviction, to harm any living thing is to do injury to the One Eternal and Divine Life. Since animals are considered to be traveling toward enlightenment just as man is, neither are they to be harmed, discouraged, or hampered in their progress. To accept the Buddhist point of view is to have a new spirit of compassion for any form of life that is weak, helpless, or hurt."

Buddhist mythology includes stories of creatures that are part animal and part divine, such as tales of the Garudas, giant winged birds of prey who protect sacred Buddhist sites from attacks by serpent-like beings called Nagas. Both the Garudas and Nagas are crafty and intelligent. Their eternal struggle exemplifies the conflict between heaven and earth.

The Snow Lion adorns the Tibetan National Flag, symbolizing fearless joy. Tibetan prayer flags contain images of the Snow Lion as well as the Tiger, for confidence; the Dragon, for gentle power; and the Garuda, for wisdom.

# Christian Denominations

*"I believe that God is the tender, loving, merciful Creator of
all things. I love Cynthia Rylant's book,* Cat Heaven,
*because when the cats in heaven are hungry, they all are
fed on 'God's kitchen counter.' (And it's okay for them to
be up there! God is not particularly concerned about
kitchen protocol.) When the cats are called to heaven, they
'curl up with God in the sky.' God wants us to do the same
for the creatures he has entrusted to our care."*

—LORI SCOTT FOGLEMAN

**SACRED TEXT(S):** *New Testament*

**BELIEF ABOUT ANIMALS:** *Animals are part of God's creation and
should be treated with love and respect. Jesus "turned over the
tables" of those who sold pigeons for sacrifice in the Temple,
virtually decrying animal sacrifice as a form of worship.*

**PRACTICE AND RITUAL:** *Annual Blessing of the Animals in various denominations.*

The annual Blessing of the Animals (related to the Feast
of St. Francis) is now celebrated by many Lutherans, Episco-
palians, Anglicans, Methodists, and the United Church of
Christ. When it comes to pets, there seems to be increasing
fellowship among Christian and non-Christian faiths.

Carolyn Cain, author of *Come Aboard the Steward Ship: Workbook*, says that Episcopal teachings on "stewardship" emphasize the importance of living in harmony with animals. In addition, liturgies of the Anglican Church often cite Psalm 148, verses 7 and 10, which beautifully describes the spiritual importance of animals: "Praise the Lord from the earth, you great sea creatures and all ocean depths; wild animals and all cattle, small creatures and flying birds."

The soulful teachings of Jesus, and his love of mankind, extend to animals. Christians believe that Jesus watches over their pets as he watches over them. Ministers from many Christian denominations have embraced their flock's need to include their pets in spiritual life and have created animal-inclusive rituals and ceremonies to satisfy those needs.

# Goddess- and Earth-Based Traditions

*"I believe Aries is my familiar. We're woven together.*
*I know when there is something wrong and so does he.*
*I prepare baths for him when he's sick, and clean his spirit*
*of things so that nothing will attach itself to him.*
*We take care of each other, in the ways we know."*

—KATHLEEN VERA

**SACRED TEXT(S):** *Oral traditions and Redes*
**BELIEF ABOUT ANIMALS:** *That they are familiars, healers, and guides, a part of the circle of life.*
**PRACTICE AND RITUAL:** *Animals are sacred. Pets are often included in rituals and honored for their wisdom, guidance, and abilities. There are many deities who are animals or who shape-shift from animal to human form.*

The ancient Goddess religions, as well as current practitioners of paganism and earth-based spirituality, honor all that the Goddess has created, including her animals and the pets she brings into our lives.

Goddess worship is based on working with the energies, elements, and essence of nature, so pets are a significant part of the spiritual experience. Most Goddess traditions and earth-based traditions include the psychic connection between human and "familiar"—an animal who helps the practitioner forge and maintain a spiritual connection to nature. Familiars are often considered healer-helpers and sources of wisdom. They offer insight and clarity because they can see those things that human eyes cannot.

In this context, cats become companion healers, and dogs are protectors on the deepest psychic levels. They often communicate, through their actions, things we don't pick up. For example, a dog may bark or growl at someone you let in your home to signal that this person cannot be trusted. A normally friendly cat might disappear and hide, telling you that this person has negative energy to be avoided. A bird may squawk. On the deeper levels, they transmit the insight to us telepathically.

Goddesses of the world traditions have often relied on their animal familiars to increase their power and enhance their abilities. Athena, the Greek Goddess of war and commerce, always had her owl on her shoulder and relied on it as an adviser. The Greek Goddess Artemis would spend all her days with her animals in the woods; they and the nymphs were her main companions, and she was perhaps the original animal communicator, as they whispered the secrets of the forest to her. Freya, the Norse Goddess of war and sexuality, had a companion cat who was protector and guide. The ancient deity known as Lady of the Beasts was an aspect of ancient Hebrew and Mesopotamian Goddesses. She gathered her sacred animals and was the mother and nurturer of all. In the ancient earth-based religions, the Great Goddess, also thought of as Mother Earth and Mother of All things, was believed to have brought forth this planet and all its creatures.

# Egyptian Religion (Ancient)

*"Believing in reincarnation has led me to the conclusion that I had two Egyptian past lives. One of those lives I was a temple priestess for Bast, the cat-headed Goddess. I definitely have a past-life thing for cats. Cats in general will respond to me on their own accord. They are drawn to me."*

—JEAN MARIE

**SACRED TEXT(S):** *The Books of Thoth and other ancient writings*

**BELIEF ABOUT ANIMALS:** *Egyptian mythology is rich with stories of divine animal beings.*

**PRACTICE AND RITUAL:** *Many major deities from this tradition were seen as human forms with animal heads and thus the related animals were worshiped. Ibis was sacred because it represented the God Thoth.*

Animals were central to the religious life of ancient Egyptians, who worshiped dozens of deities that appeared as humans with heads in the image of animals. Major gods included Thoth, an ibis; Horus, a falcon; Sehkmet, a lion; and Anubis, a jackal who watched over the underworld.

Bast or Bastet, the Cat Goddess, was the Egyptian Goddess of play, pleasure, frolic, fun, music, dancing, and celebration. She was the ruler of the holy city of Bubastis in Lower Egypt, which was devoted to all of those playful qualities—and to cats. Almost everyone in Bubastis had a cat. Bast was so cherished by her people that cats were considered sacred creatures, bejeweled by their owners in life and mummified like humans in death. In addition, many of the Bubastic temples bred sacred cats that lived like royalty inside the temple, worshiped as the personification of Bast here on Earth. Her feast day was celebrated with unbridled enthusiasm each year.

Many mummified animals have been found in ancient Egyptian tombs. Egyptians believed in the afterlife and took their worldly goods and their favorite animals with them on the journey.

There are still many modern spiritual followers who embrace this ancient religion, and Bast continues in her place of honor, along with her companion animal Goddesses and Gods.

# Hinduism

*"I believe that animals bring messages to us from God."*

—KRISTEN GABRIEL

**SACRED TEXT(S):** *Vedas (oral tradition), Upanishads (written commentaries on the Vedas)*
**BELIEF ABOUT ANIMALS:** *All animals are considered sacred, and several are worshiped as deities.*
**PRACTICE AND RITUAL:** *The elephant-headed deity, Ganesha, is worshiped as the overcomer of obstacles. Cows are revered and protected from harm.*

A *puja* is one of the major forms of worship in the Hindu tradition. In this service the Gods and Goddesses are honored and celebrated with chanting, singing, ghee candles, incense, and offerings of food—fruit, yogurt, and milk—and flowers. Quite colorful, and often loud, it is filled with chanting that is said to open one's consciousness. There are special *pujas* for honoring animals big and small.

The Hindu tradition is known for great reverence for animals. Most Hindus are vegetarians and we can thank that culture for the expression "sacred cow." Essential to the religion is worship of Gods in the image of animals.

"Hindus see divinity in all living creatures," according

to the Hindu Universe, a Hindu resource center at www.hindunet.org. "Animal deities therefore, occupy an important place in Hindu dharma. Animals, for example, are a very common form of transport for various Gods and Goddesses. Animals also appear as independent divine creatures."

Lord Hanuman, one of the heroes of the epic *Ramayana*, has a man's body with the head of a monkey. And Lord Vishnu, the Great Preserver, incarnates as the cowherd avatar Krishna, as a fish, and as a turtle. A major deity is Ganesha, the elephant-headed God, son of Lord Shiva and Goddess Parvati. Ganesha, as Lord of Success and Remover of Obstacles, is always the first God evoked in the Hindu tradition.

# Islam

*"I believe that animals have souls and can feel love."*

—ANGELA DRINKWATER

**SACRED TEXT(S):** *Qur'an*
**BELIEF ABOUT ANIMALS:** *Animals are to be treated with kindness and dignity.*
**PRACTICE AND RITUAL:** *None*

Islam has always viewed animals as a special part of Allah's creation.

The Qur'an and Hadith both contain examples of kindness and compassion toward animals. Muslims believe that Allah has given them the role of guardians of all living things. Therefore they hold it their duty, as Muslims, to protect and cherish Allah's earth. Muslims believe they have a certain responsibility toward the earth and the creatures on it, including animals, which Allah has given to be used appropriately and wisely. Islam teaches that mercy and compassion should be shown to animals.

In Qur'an, 88:17, nonbelievers are admonished to reflect upon the camel and how it was perfectly created to survive in the desert and be of service as evidence of God's miracles. "Do they not look at the Camels, how they are made?"

There is a difference of opinion among Muslims as to the ownership of pets, particularly dogs. The Qur'an makes several references to dogs dwelling with humans and to the loving relationship between them. According to the Islamic Web site www.submission.org, false *hadiths* (commentaries) by Abu Hurayra contradicted the Qur'an and said that dogs were undesirable. This is said to have led to the belief by many Muslims that dogs were not suitable as pets.

# Judaism

*"I believe that animals are gifts from God sent into our lives for specific purposes. Often you will have a pet that seems more human than most humans. I consider these to be tiny, furry spirit guides. My dog Max came to me seemingly with the knowledge of our family rituals. It was as if God (or my previous dog on the other side) had given him instructions before he joined our family."*

—CAROLE MUMFORD

**SACRED TEXT(S):** *Torah, Talmud*

**BELIEF ABOUT ANIMALS:** *Humanity is the steward of all animals, and animals should be treated with kindness and dignity. Animals are recognized as having souls.*

**PRACTICE AND RITUAL:** *Kosher laws prescribe humane slaughter. Cruelty to animals is prohibited. In Orthodox Judaism, animals "rest from work" on the sabbath as humans do. Animals are required to be fed before humans eat.*

Judaism offers both traditional and mystical ways of viewing our relationship with our pets. Caring for an animal and taking in a stray could be considered a *mitzvah* (a commandment) in the Jewish tradition because it is an act of kindness and caring, a good deed.

In Genesis 1:26, we see the foundation of humankind's relationship with animals when God creates Adam and gives him "dominion" over them. The Hebrew word for dominion, *radah*, implies rule in the highest senses of mercy, caring, and compassion.

This tradition continues throughout the Hebrew Bible as we see many of the great leaders, including Moses and David, depicted as shepherds caring for their flocks.

Genesis 1:21 uses the word *nefesh*, or soul, in conjunction with the creation of animals, indicating that animals, like human beings, are living souls.

Jewish law is very specific as to the relationship between humans and animals. Animals are to be treated with compassion and concern, they must be fed before their human masters; and even though they may be used for food, clothing, and work, it is forbidden to cause them unnecessary pain and stress.

# Native American
# and Shamanic Traditions

*"As a true nature spirit myself, I know my dogs are direct
spirit guides parading around as four-footed creatures with
fur. While I don't espouse any particular belief system other
than Love, I recognize their wisdom as clear and direct,
and plummeting gently toward all of us as a feather that
floats by direct from the universe, God inspired. God. Dog.
There is a relationship!"*

—DR. LAUREN NAPPEN

**SACRED TEXT(S):** *Various oral traditions*
**BELIEF ABOUT ANIMALS:** *Animals are symbols and guides
through the cycles of life. Animals are "people" who are four-
legged or winged.*
**PRACTICE AND RITUAL:** *Working with our totem animals as
guides on our spiritual journey.*

The Native American tradition adheres to the belief in the
interconnectedness of all of creation. We humans are seen
as stewards of the earth and all her children. There is a
Lakota chant that tells us "Earth is our mother; we must take
care of her."

This tradition holds that every living thing has a spirit. Animals are often referred to as people, and in endearing terms such as "the four-legged," "the winged ones," "the ones who swim," or "the ones who crawl the earth." One of the most powerful aspects of Native American and some indigenous shamanic traditions is "animal medicine," based on the belief that each animal has special qualities to impart to us and special guidance and wisdom to offer. It also teaches that we each have five totem animals, which represent us and influence us.

The Indian legends and myths tell countless tales of talking animals and animals who do amazing things. One story tells how the Coyote, who wanted to bring the gift of fire to his two-legged friends, craftily stole a burning ember from the selfish Fire Beings and gave it to humanity. Shamanic traditions around the world have held that animals were directly conversant with the "Great Spirit" and brought knowledge and wisdom to humanity.

# Roman Catholicism

*"When you welcome a dog, or any animal or being into your life, you don't know what you are really in for. But with animals it's not right to call it quits. It happens, though. As adoptive dog parents, we benefited from someone else's wrong."*

—MEGHAN AND NATE McVAY

**SACRED TEXT(S):** *New Testament*
**BELIEF ABOUT ANIMALS:** *Does not hold that animals have souls, according to argument given by St. Thomas Aquinas in his* Summa Theologica. *Catechism teaches that animals are God's creatures and should be treated with kindness.*
**PRACTICE AND RITUAL:** *Feast of St. Francis of Assisi, annual blessings of the animals.*

The Roman Catholic tradition knows how to bless animals well and opens its doors to pets of all faiths in churches that celebrate the Feast of St. Francis (October 4 or thereabout). The Scriptures are rich with mentions of animals. Remember Genesis? "You shall have dominion over the fish of the sea, dominion over the birds of the Heavens, over all the Earth, over every creeping thing that creepeth upon the Earth." And Noah's Ark, where representatives of the animal world are spared in pairs. Jesus is known as The Good Shepherd and often pictured with a lamb. Although the Bible has more to say about donkeys than about dogs or gerbils, Proverbs 12:10 teaches that "The righteous man regards the life of his beast."

Catholicism, however, departs from the Jewish belief about animals having "living souls." St. Thomas Aquinas in his *Summa Theologica* refutes this concept, saying that since animals do not display intellect, they lack souls in the human sense.

# All Creatures Great and Small

Annual blessings of the animals are a Christian tradition that has filtered into the mainstream. They are becoming an interfaith and nondenominational experience as more and more pet owners bring their pets out simply because it can never hurt to have too many blessings!

Every year, on or around October 4, churches around the world celebrate the feast day of St. Francis, patron saint of animals, by inviting parishioners, neighbors, and the public to bring their pets for a special blessing.

Catholic churches, as well as other Christian and nondenominational churches, are traditional hosts. We've heard of everything from blessings on the beach in Los Angeles to animal prayers on the streets of Louisiana during Katrina search and rescue. The shelter where we found Kismet has a clergyperson on call who regularly blesses the animals that desperately need homes.

In the same way that the Pope blesses cars from the window of the Vatican, and a church in Manhattan blesses actors who are out of work with a prayer that they get jobs, public pet prayers go out to people of all faiths as well as the unaffiliated, agnostics, and people who would not ordinarily give religion the time of day.

We observed many different services while researching

this book and we feel that regardless of the denomination, partaking in the blessing of the animals is a wonderful way for you and your pet to experience the universal language of pet prayers. If your pet is ill and can't travel, try bringing a photo. An open-minded clergyperson might be willing to bless your pet via the photo.

In the numerous services we visited, we found that most priests and ministers used very general language. Often the blessing is held outside the church—for obvious reasons, but also because it makes it easier for *all* pet owners to partake. You won't have to walk into a house of worship that may not be yours; you can hang out in God's country—nature—with your pet.

In our neighborhood, outside a Catholic church, two priests formed a blessing line. One joked, "This line is for the friendly dogs that do not bite." They offered brief blessings, with the sign of the cross. It was not a big "religious" deal: *Fido, may you be loved and may you live the life that God has put you on this earth to fulfill . . . in the name of the Father, the Son, and the Holy Spirit.*

At a Methodist church, we saw the minister ask the owners what specific blessings their animals needed. He got down on the ground with the dogs, petting them and playing with them. Each animal was blessed in the same spirit but with different intentions.

These animal blessings are often "light" on religion and big on spirit. In many ways, it is not so much a religious experience as it is an experience of noticing how joyful it is to include pets. Besides, it is fun to see people line up with pooches, turtles, guinea pigs, birds, cats, snakes, ferrets, and others. It is also a chance for pets—and their humans—to socialize.

The camaraderie among pet owners makes it even more fun. They may be people from all walks, yet they share a common experience—a love of their pets that is so deep that they want them to be blessed and honored! So keep your eyes open for the blessing of the animals in your neighborhood.

One of the most famous is at the Cathedral Church of St. John the Divine, the famed Gothic cathedral in New York City. It's a New York tradition that draws people and animals from far and wide. Our friend Reverend Sandra Lee Schubert has long been affiliated with the Cathedral and shares her experience on page 38.

# Pet Tale:

## *The Greatest Animal Blessing on Earth*

BY REVEREND SANDRA LEE SCHUBERT

The annual feast of St. Francis at the Cathedral Church of St. John the Divine in Manhattan is like no other. The Cathedral is a grand and magnificent space. It easily holds three thousand people. Imagine that many people, and their pets, *and* a worship service. Here, on the first weekend of October every year, the earthly and the divine meet in one incredible moment.

The space allows for majestic meanderings and gleeful surges of rapture. Where else could an elephant, a camel, and oxen be dwarfed by the space they are in?

The Cathedral fills to capacity with every kind of creature. There are huge pot-bellied pigs, big dogs, tiny kittens, snakes, and birds. You can only imagine what it might have been like to live in the ark, filled with the sounds and smells of so many animals. This cacophony resounds off the walls, and the cathedral is a massive carnival of giddy children with their tiny pets and stuffed animals. The first time I witnessed it, I was wholly unprepared for this chaos and even less prepared for the service itself.

In the midst of this noise and activity the organ begins to

play and, as if given some secret signal, the animals become quiet. Starting from the very back, the procession begins; acolytes, priests, and animals join this great throng of people and pets. There are banners representing the elements of our common being (air, earth, fire, water), and behind each banner is a representative of a species. Air brings birds, from the tiny sparrow to the magnificent eagle. Water brings fishes and turtles and frogs. Earth brings dogs and oxen and camels. Even the lowly earth worm makes an appearance. Adding to the festive air, artist-in-residence Paul Winter, along with the Paul Winter Consort and the resident dancers, offer dazzling musical and dance performances.

Most people bring their cats and dogs with the occasional talking parrot on its owner's shoulder, yet you may find yourself sitting next to a family, each holding a python; on the other side of them is a little girl with her gerbil. Behind her is a family that has brought their stuffed animals. Next to them is a woman who has dressed her two dogs up in matching outfits. Anything goes, and any pet is welcome.

This annual blessing was the vision of the late John-Michael Tebelak, creator of *Godspell*. Inspired by the life and work of St. Francis of Assisi, who insisted on harmony with the natural world, it is not just about blessing animals; it is honoring what has been created. Since the first festival in 1985, clergy have blessed thousands of creatures, including a turkey vulture, a skunk, a python, chimpanzees, donkeys, worms, algae, and a 3.5-billion-year-old Australian fossil. Human participants have included Vice President Al Gore, Dr. Carl Sagan, and other luminaries.

After the service the fun continues while owners and pets receive personal blessings on the grounds of the Cathedral. There is food—vegetarian, of course—and music and games for the children. There is a contest for owners and pets. Animals can be adopted from local rescue organizations, doggie sweaters are for sale, and owners mingle with one another and their Great Danes and kittens. Truly it is a great carnival, a blessing not just for the animals but for us all.

*The Annual Feast of St. Francis is held the first Sunday each October at the Cathedral of Saint John the Divine, located at 1047 Amsterdam Avenue just north of 110th Street. 212-316-7490, http://www.stjohndivine.org*

# Part One
## Summary Prayer

Whether my pet is large or small,

No matter the breed or species,

Or whether we are religious at all,

Let us find ways to live spiritually with the animals we love.

Let us bless them.

Let us pray for them.

Let us share ceremony and celebrations with them.

Let us find our own personal approach to

creating pet prayers and blessings.

# Part Two

*Prayers and Rituals for Starting
Your New Life Together*

"I always have ceremonies to honor my pets.
Whenever I get a new pet, or an animal finds me, I
present the animal to each element within my sacred
area, and ask for protection for them . . . against other
animals, sickness, and, of course, cars. I involve my pets
in any ritual I may be doing, or they sit with me while
I meditate. Usually, they are well behaved."

—MYSTL

# Chapter Three

*Welcoming Your Pet to Your World*

Every spiritual tradition has a way of blessing new babies and welcoming them into the world. Why not bless and bestow this kind of sweet welcoming upon your new pet(s)? Here we offer a variety of different ways you can create welcoming, naming, and blessing rituals for your new pets. You can choose to do this along with a gathering or party, or make it an intimate moment with just close family members.

**TO PREPARE FOR A SMOOTH CEREMONY:**

- *Select a time of day when your pet is more sociable or likely to be more relaxed.*
- *Make sure to feed your pet a snack beforehand and make sure he or she has visited the restroom.*
- *Keep the animal's stress level low (for example, if you have a shy pooch or a newly rescued cat, don't invite fifty guests).*

- *If you are having guests, ask them to arrive at a specific time.*
- *Ask family to gather at a specific time as well.*
- *Select a part of the room/house where the blessing will take place.*
- *Set up your "altar table" (can be any table or flat surface) and ritual supplies such as candles in advance.*
- *Decide if guests will stand or sit, and set up the room accordingly.*
- *Know in advance who will lead the ceremony and who will have a role in it—such as offering a blessing or holding the pet.*
- *Have a copy of the ceremony or this book in hand.*
- *If a meal or reception is to follow, have everything ready to go immediately following the ceremony.*

# Welcoming and Blessing Ceremony for Our Puppy, Kismet

(can be adapted to any pet)

**HOW TO PREPARE:**

- *Have a small tabletop or table available as altar.*
- *Provide a CD player, MP3 player, or iPod.*
- *Pre-select music.*
- *Place one white votive candle and matches on the table.*
- *Choose a treat for the pet, to be given at the end of the ceremony.*

## OPENING REMARKS

Thank you all for being here. The "new baby" in this home is our Kismet, and we want to take a moment to welcome the four-legged one who has become part of our family. She is a blessing in our lives. Let us create—together—a sacred space. We begin with a piece of music.

**SUGGESTED MUSIC:** "Circle of Life," from *The Lion King*; "You'll Be in My Heart," from *Tarzan*, something Disney or Doggy.

## OPENING INVOCATION

*Divine Spirit of all there is,*
*Please fill this place with your loving presence . . .*
*Cast a circle of love and light around us all*
*And guide us in making these moments sacred and fun*
*as we bless and celebrate this unique soul, Kismet. Amen.*

## CANDLE LIGHTING

*Pet's parent(s) light a candle for the new addition and say:*
*This candle celebrates Kismet, the new light in our hearts and*
*in this home.*
*This candle celebrates the sunshine she will bring to our lives*
*and to the world around her.*
*This candle celebrates the joy we feel to have her companionship.*

## CLOSING PRAYER

*This animal is a child of Divine Spirit, as we all are.*
*May her life be filled with security and trust.*
*May her days be long.*
*May her health be good.*
*May her heart be happy.*
*May she love and be loved each day of her life.*

## TO GUESTS

On behalf of Kismet and her family, thank you all for being here. May love and joy fill your hearts as you enjoy the celebratory feast that follows.

We end with a special treat for Kismet.
*(Give her a doggie treat or something yummy, and end with music and merriment!)*

# Naming Ceremony

**HOW TO PREPARE:**

- Write out your pet's name vertically, and next to each letter of the pet's name write a related blessing.
- Keep the blessing handy and ready to read.
- Have a "godparent" or designated family member hold the animal during the blessing.

Be creative and have fun, and use this naming ceremony to honor the good qualities in your pet as well as to imbue your pet with desired qualities. This can be adapted for any kind of pet, using any name. Just take each letter of the name and embellish it to give the name a deeper meaning. Here is an example: a naming ceremony created for a kitten named Flora.

## OPENING REMARKS

There is a beautiful Kabbalistic tradition we use to celebrate children of all faiths. Today we evoke this tradition for our new furry baby, Flora. It is a tradition that tells us to take each letter in the given name and embellish it with qualities and traits that empower and suit the special soul you are naming.

**F IS FOR FUN AND FROLICKING.** May you enjoy this life to the fullest, having fun as you frolic along your merry way, entertaining yourself and us, and reminding us what it is to be playful!

**L IS FOR LOVE.** May your life and your little heart be filled with it always! And may you be surrounded by the love of those who care for you.

**O IS FOR OWNER.** May you be blessed with delightful pet parents devoted to you and willing to care for you in every way.

**R IS FOR RESISTANCE.** May you resist tearing, shredding, and scratching at things your owners love and instead use your scratching post.

**A IS FOR ADORABLE.** May you always be as adorable and sweet as you are today! As you grow, we pray that you keep your youthful spirit and always enjoy the life you have.

## PARTING SENTIMENT

We bestow Flora with this creative interpretation of her name. In doing so, may we imbue her life with these qualities. And so it is!

# Welcome a Pet into a New Home with a Blessing of the Elements

**HOW TO PREPARE:**

- *Organize guests in a circle, Native American-style, either sitting in chairs, sitting on the floor, or standing.*
- *Prepare an altar with small items representing the elements: a rock or crystal for earth, a feather for wind, a candle for fire, a pet bowl with water representing water, and so forth.*
- *Call together the animal and any family members involved in this blessing.*

This ritual can be conducted by one person who reads and five friends and family who can each partake by lifting one of the elements over the pet's head or rubbing the pet's belly.

This is a special blessing taken from the Native American earth traditions. It is a strong petition that your pet be guided and protected from all directions and by the elements of our common being.

*Gently lift each element above the animal's head as the related blessing is spoken:*

*Divine Spirit of all there is, we honor all you have created, especially the elements of our common being. And today we honor the four-legged (or flying or swimming) one we have brought into our home.*

*Help us welcome this new being, embrace her/him into our hearth and home. We ask for your blessings for this new pet.*

*We honor Mother Earth and ask that this pet be one with Mother Nature and grow stronger with each season.*
*(Lift rock or crystals, then return to altar)*
*We honor the east and wind and ask that this pet have a smooth sail through life.*
*(Lift feather, then return to altar)*
*We honor the south and fire and ask that this pet be warm in our loving embrace.*
*(Lift candle, then return to altar)*
*We honor the west and water and ask that this pet never thirst or go hungry.*
*(Lift water, then return to altar)*
*We honor the spirit within and ask that this pet be balanced and healthy and happy in this home.*
*(Touch pet's solar plexus, mid-belly)*
*We honor heaven and earth, and all the forces of the universe; we pray for harmony and joy as this pet grows young with us.*
*(Pause)*
*Thank you, Divine Spirit of all Directions and Elements, for blessing our pet. And so it is.*

# Water Blessings

## NONDENOMINATIONAL BLESSING
## WITH WATER

**HOW TO PREPARE:**

- *Bless the water yourself using a small bottle of spring water.*
- *Hold it between two hands as you allow your heart and mind to fill with beautiful blessings for your pet.*
- *Then hold it to your heart and say: "I bless this water in the name of love."*
- *Pour a small amount of this water in a designated, special cup.*
- *Have the cup of water ready at the altar.*

Anoint the animal's third eye—center of forehead—with pure or blessed water and/or dip your fingertips into the water three times and sprinkle water to the left, center, and right of your pet. If caged or in a tank, sprinkle to the left, center, and right of the tank or cage.

*Say: We bless you in the spirit of love, joy, and welcoming. Always know how much you are wanted and adored!*

After the ceremony, give the water to your pet to drink—offer a few sips from the cup or pour it into a fresh drinking bowl. (For a fish, pour blessed water into the tank only if you can properly treat it first.)

# PET BAPTISMAL BLESSING

**HOW TO PREPARE:**

- *Follow the instruction from Nondenominational Blessing with Water.*
- *Bless your own water or use holy water from your house of worship.*

Dip your fingertips into the water three times and sprinkle water to the left, center, and right of your pet.

*Say: In the name of the Father, the Son, and the Holy Spirit, we baptize and bless this animal.*
*God of light and love*
*Please welcome this pet as a being of your light,*
*Please bless his/her life so that he/she can*
*Live the life God created for her/him.*
*Almighty, ever-loving God,*
*Let your hand guide this animal.*
*Let your holy spirit be with him/her, evermore.*
*We ask this in the name of the Father, the Son, and the Holy Spirit, through your son, Jesus Christ.*
*And we all say, Amen.*

# Chapter Four

*Blessing the New Abode*

It is important to welcome your pet to his or her new home by blessing the place, or places, in which the animal will dwell or spend much of its time.

For pets that are contained, you will have a smaller, more specific area to bless. For pets who will roam and move about with their human family, it is helpful to spiritually introduce the animal to each part of the house and gently set the ground rules.

You can adapt the following blessings to the kind of pet you have, and you can personalize the blessings with your own sentiments.

# *Welcome to Your World:*

## FENG SHUI BLESSING OF INTENT

**HOW TO PREPARE:**
*Make sure candle and matches are on a safe surface.*
*If this is a furry pet (or slithery or flying friend) that will move*
*around on their own, gently walk or carry the pet through*
*every room of the house and welcome him or her to his new*
*abode while gently laying down the boundaries.*

## LIGHT CANDLE AND STATE YOUR INTENT

Before you begin, light a candle (safely, where it will not get knocked over) and offer a "statement of intent," speaking words of welcome to your pet while also asking for the animal's assistance in maintaining balance and order in the home.

*We welcome you to this house.*
*This home is now your home.*
*We invite you to be part of our family.*
*We want to love you with all our hearts.*
*And we want you to roam free, as it is your nature.*
*We ask only you to be respectful of what we have built.*
*We promise to provide you with all you need.*
*Please resist temptation to take more than is offered.*
*Please do all you can to follow our rules.*

*Please let us love each other and live in peace.*
*We welcome you to this house.*

Then begin the walking tour of your home, and offering your "blessing of intent." Here are some examples we used with our dog, Kismet. You can adapt as needed.

**THIS IS THE BACKYARD.** We built this fence for you so you can run and jump and enjoy yourself outside. This is your special space. We hope this helps you stay connected to nature and your home in Louisiana.

*Backyard Blessing: May you feel secure yet free as you explore nature in the backyard.*

**THIS IS OUR LIVING ROOM.** We entertain here and this is where Mom does much of her work. Please do not bark or jump on the clients who come to see her. We would appreciate it if you would refrain from destroying the leather couch. Please enjoy the bay window, which will allow you to look out into the world as you get used to your new one. We honor your "watchdog" qualities, but if you could keep the barking at neighbors down, we'd appreciate it.

*Living Room Blessing: May this room offer a window on the world that connects your senses to the outdoors, and may you feel secure as you keep Mom company all through the day.*

**THIS IS OUR FAMILY ROOM.** We relax here. You may enter this room at any time and hang out with us. Enjoy the couch, but please don't eat the TV remote (again).

*Family Room Blessing: May this room offer a warm embrace to you, as it does for all of us.*

**THIS IS OUR KITCHEN.** We gather here to eat and spend time as a family. You are part of our family, too, so we welcome you to join us. Your food is on the floor (or wherever the pet's food is) and ours is on the table. It is important that we all get the nutrition most appropriate to each of us, and that we not mix our food with yours.

*Kitchen Blessing: May you trust that we will feed you the food that is best for you and may you thrive on family time and good meals.*

**THIS IS OUR BATHROOM.** This is where we wash and cleanse, and where we do our "business." (If the animal's litter box, pee pad, or other will be located in that room, explain.) Please don't drink from the toilet or lick water from our toes when we get out of the shower, but feel free to keep us company at bath time.

*Bathroom Blessing: May you easily deal with your own toileting needs in all appropriate ways. AMEN!*

**THIS IS OUR BEDROOM.** This is where we sleep at night; and as much as we love you, we would like to keep our bed a dog-hair-free zone. Please understand that we don't want to develop allergies or itches that would cause us to have to reconsider having a dog. You are allowed in all other rooms but this one.

> *Master Bedroom Blessing: May you know you are loved and adored, even though we do not allow you on our bed or in our bedroom.*

**THIS IS ALEXANDER'S BEDROOM.** This is where he sleeps, talks on the phone, watches ball games, and does homework. He loves you so much. That is why we found you: for Alex. We want you to be able to hang out in his room and eventually sleep on his bed, but you must show us you can be a good doggy and quit chewing his bed, bedpost, pillows, and him.

> *Alex's Bedroom Blessing: May you be a wonderful companion to the boy who rescued you from the shelter and took you home to be his best friend.*

**THIS IS KISMET'S SPECIAL PLACE.** Your bedroom is the foyer that connects our bedroom and Alexander's so you can be close to all of us. Your special place is the big crate we got to keep you cozy, until the time when you do not poop on the floor or tear things up in the night. It is right in front of Alexander's room, and secure against two walls. We will always tuck you into bed with water and a treat, so please settle in when we call "bedtime." And please protect our boy as he sleeps. That is one of your special jobs.

*Kismet's Crate and Special Place Blessing: May you feel close and connected to us all, your family, as we slumber.*

# *Blessing for Your Pet's Special Place*

## INCLUDING TURTLES AND GERBILS
## AND SNAKES, OH MY!

Like humans, pets need their sacred space—a place to call their own.

Some animals will have their own little apartment in your home in the form of a tank. Some will have special cages. Perhaps they will have cat or dog beds, or crates. It is appropriate to bless any specific environment in which your pet will spend time. Bless also the things that are part of the environment—the hamster's play wheel, the bird's toy, the dog's treat, for example. Obviously, each kind of pet will have different needs, but they will share the common need for food, water, shelter, love, and caring from you.

## BLESSINGS FOR A FISH TANK

*All kinds of fish*

*We bless this fish tank.*

*May it be a healthy, happy home for you.*

*May you thrive and grow as you swim around.*

*May the filter bubbles be just right.*

*And may the oxygen level be perfect for your needs.*

*We promise to keep this tank clean for you*

*and fill it with the right kind water*
*and the correct amount/type of food.*
*We will do out best not to agitate you when we clean your water.*
*May you gently flow through your days on earth*
*and be happy here.*
*This is our blessing for you.*

## BLESSINGS FOR A TANK
*For turtle, reptile, snake, gerbil, hamster, or guinea pig tanks.
*We bless this tank.*
*May it be a healthy, happy home for you.*
*May you thrive and grow and enjoy your time here.*
*May it supply all the food, drink, oxygen, and joy*
*you need to live a full life.*
*We promise to fulfill all your needs here*
*and keep this place clean for you.*
*We will interact with you as much as possible,*
*and will handle you gently when*
*taking you out into the open air to play.*
*May your days on earth be long and happy here.*
*This is our blessing for you.*

## BLESSING FOR A BIRD CAGE

*For birds

We bless this cage.

May it be a healthy, happy home for you.

May you thrive and grow and enjoy your time here.

May it supply all the food, drink, oxygen, and joy
you need to live a full life.

May this be a place that fills all your needs.

May you enjoy your little swing, and toys.

May the bird seed be to your liking.

We will let you out to stretch your wings
as much as possible,
and will handle you gently when
putting you back into your cage.

May your days on earth be long and happy here.

This is our blessing for you.


## BLESSING FOR A CAGE

*For rabbit and ferret cages

We bless this cage.

May it be a healthy, happy home for you.

May you thrive and grow and enjoy your time here.

May it supply all the food, drink, oxygen, and joy
you need to live a full life.

May this be a place that fills all your needs.
We will interact with you as much as possible,
and will handle you gently when
taking you out into the open air.
We will let you run around and stretch and play,
and ask only that, if you get away somewhere in the house,
that you come back soon!
May your days on earth be long and happy here.
This is our blessing for you.


## BLESSING FOR A CAT OR DOG BED/CRATE

*For the four-legged ones who roam the home
We bless this bed (this rug, this special place, this crate).
May it be a place you love to lay your head and dream.
May it make you feel secure, in your own special place.
After roaming around and playing,
may you always enjoy the return to your sanctuary,
a place that is yours alone.
May this special resting place uphold you when you are sleepy,
and give you refuge when you need your space.
During the days and nights
we will interact with you in many ways,
we will let you run around and stretch and play,
then we will always respect your sacred space.

*When it is time for bed,*
*and the night falls like a curtain around our home,*
*we will hope to see you comfortably nestled in your bed.*
*May it bring your comfort and peace.*
*This is our blessing for you.*

# Pet Tale:

*Lucy the Cat*

BY GAY HENDRICKS

One of the most precious relationships of my life is with our cat, Lucy. We found each other ten years ago, and from the moment she entered our lives she has been pure joy. Lucy has so much presence and such a refined consciousness that my wife, Kathlyn, and I long ago ceased to think of her as a pet. We think of her as a boon companion who came into our lives by grace. She's also a teacher who helps me see more clearly how life really works. I love her dearly.

We decided to get a cat as a Christmas present to ourselves in 1995, our first year in Santa Barbara. We lived at the time just a block away from a pet shop on the main street of Montecito. Passing by the shop one day, we saw a beautiful gray Persian reclining majestically in the window. She was so captivatingly regal that we went inside to take a closer look. Frances, the cat with the queenly presence, was the owner's pride and joy, and she was *definitely* not for sale (said the owner with an indignant glare). However, we found that Frances had just delivered what was to be her last litter. There were five kittens, and if we came back in two weeks they would be ready for adoption. The owner named an outrageous price. She wagged her finger and added that the price was nonnegotiable. I had never bought a cat before, but my impression was it was something you did for ten bucks at an animal shelter. Not in Montecito, though. Still, we couldn't get Frances off our minds, so two weeks later we went back to the shop to see the kittens.

We went downstairs into the basement room where they were playing. We stood quietly by the door, watching five madcap bundles of gray fur ricocheting around the room. One of them, a big male, actually crashed into my legs, picked himself up, and dashed off again. In a moment, though, a bit of magic happened. A petite girl-kitten came jogging over to us, took a seat on her haunches, and looked up at us with the clearest gaze and the sweetest face imaginable. Katie and I both laughed out loud and felt our hearts melt.

"Looks like we found our kitten," I said. I reached down and scooped her up gently.

"Or she found us," Katie said.

Suddenly the price seemed irrelevant, a bargain even. We took Lucy up the road to her new home, and thus began our wonderful lives together.

A definitive event occurred the first night Lucy was with us. We'd been playing with her nonstop all evening (during which she collapsed in a heap for a few quick catnaps), so by bedtime Katie and I were zonked. We went to sleep around 11 P.M., after getting Lucy settled in her cat-bed. We dropped off to sleep right away, but in the middle of the night, I became aware of another presence in our bed. I woke up and looked to my right. There was one of most charming sights I'd ever seen. Lucy had come to bed with us and was stretched out with her little body under the covers and her head sticking out, just like us. And that's the way it's been every night for the nearly three thousand nights she's slept with us.

## Part Two
## Summary Prayer

*We bless this pet and welcome her/him into our home.*
*We ask for wisdom and knowledge on how to*
*care for our new pet.*
*We ask that we be guided as Pet Parents to provide the best.*
*We bless this fish tank.*
*We bless this turtle, reptile, snake, gerbil,*
*hamster, or guinea pig's tanks.*
*We bless this bird cage.*
*We bless these rabbit and ferret cages.*
*We bless this crate.*
*We bless this pet bed.*
*and we welcome this pet into a life of security*
*and love in our home.*
*And so it is!*

# Part Three

## Celebrating Good Times and Including Pets in Special Occasions

"It seems to me every day is a celebration."

—DR. LAUREN NAPPEN

"I celebrate my animal companions' birthday and anniversary by wishing them 'Happy Birthday.' I honor them on an almost daily basis for being in my life and contributing what they contribute."

—RICHARD COHEN, PHD

Our animal companions have become so much a part of our daily lives that it is natural to want to celebrate special occasions significant to their lives, and to include them in our big moments and holiday celebrations. Here are some ideas for celebrating birthdays, anniversaries, and special occasions—and yes, having a wedding for your pet, or making your beloved pet a part of yours.

# Chapter Five

*Pet Parties and Birthday Bashes*

*"We always celebrate the birthdays of our cats and if
we have a dinner party around that time guests are
asked to bring gifts. We had a family friend who made
gift cards with a pencil drawing of a mouse on the
front. On the inside, it said 'to Jupiter and Olympus
with love and respect.'"*

—DANNY AND FRED JONES

These days, many pet owners acknowledge their pet's birthday in some way.

Not everyone has the desire to throw a birthday bash for a
pet, but a little celebration might be lovely—just make sure
you do not feed Fido chocolate cake or let your pet ferret get
lost under the sink during the festivities.

# Birthday Celebrations

**HOW TO PREPARE:**

- *Decide whether you will use a blessing or a toast—or both.*
- *If you want to set forth a birthday vision, write one that is appropriate for your pet, or organize your thoughts on note cards.*
- *Prepare and organize celebratory food and goodie bags in advance.*
- *Have treats and toys to play with for invited pets.*
- *Make sure there is water for furry friends.*

While some of us are blessed to know the time and date our beloved pets came into the world, others of us must wing it with a guess. If you are not sure when your animal was born, we suggest selecting an auspicious day that is *in the vicinity* of when your vet, pet shop, or animal shelter thinks your little one came into the world.

If you are so inclined, throw a birthday party and invite people and some companion pets. (We can provide the spiritual inspiration, but please make sure you provide a safe environment.)

In addition to food for the people, make sure there are treats for your pet and any pet guests. Take plenty of photos. Later, hang one near your pet's special place in your house so he/she—actually, you!—has a happy memory at which to gaze. Here are some ways to honor your pet's birthday:

## A BIRTHDAY TOAST

*Baron, I raise my cup to you.*
*Here's wishing you a dog's (or any other animal) life.*
*Let it be filled with good health, good eats, comfy sleeping arrangements, and unlimited amusement.*

## A BIRTHDAY BLESSING

*May you live long*
*and enjoy this life.*
*May you always be nourished*
*and may you have plenty of play time.*
*May you be loved*
*and always have someone to love.*
*May you be blessed in all ways*
*by God above.*

## SETTING FORTH A BIRTHDAY VISION

This is a special vision you articulate on your pet's behalf, looking forward to the next year. It may seem slightly self-serving—because it is!—yet a relaxed pet owner makes for a happier and more balanced pet. If your pet has a sense of humor, feel free to be playful with this. If she/he is prim and proper, better tone it down. Here's one we created for Kismet.

## OUR VISION FOR KISMET

Our beloved Kismet: by next year this time, we see you as far more peaceful, and as a calm, relaxed dog.

We envision you traveling around with us to places you love—like those big green fields and beautiful bays—and also lying in the living room quietly enjoying a doggie life. By that time, we can see you smiling instead of barking, saying a quiet hello to the mailman and everyone who comes to our door.

We know you will walk calmly rather than jumping at people on bicycles, or those unsuspecting pedestrians wearing hats, who somehow set you off.

We see you getting so much exercise and play that you never have to chew another pen or drag our underwear out of the hamper for a snack.

You will be so relaxed that you will walk leisurely, side by side, rather than pulling us to the other end of the earth as you jerk forward on your leash.

Your love life will be so awesome that you will no longer nip at tiny dogs who show affection to your boyfriend, the Dalmatian in the dog park . . . Nor will you feel compelled to jump up between Mom and Dad whenever they try to kiss.

You will be so settled here with us that we will never see that crazed look you get when you haven't exercised enough. We will no longer have to eat over the sink, or have Alexander cover his dinner plate with his entire body so that you cannot get at his food.

A year from now, we see you happy, healthy, and as loving as the day we found one another. Your trauma from Katrina will be in your past, and you will know how much you are loved, and that will help you relax into life in our little house!

# Anniversary of the Day Your Pet Came to Live with You

*"On the anniversary of the day I adopted her, I would usually treat Muffin to a big juicy hamburger!"*

—MICHAEL ROSENBERG

**HOW TO PREPARE:**
- *If celebrating with others, prepare a small feast for humans and animals.*
- *Carve out some quiet contemplative time.*
- *Plan a day of fun for you and your pet.*

This is an important rite of passage and can be considered a new "birthday" for your pet because it is the day your relationship was born. You can celebrate with others, or quietly with the family, or just you and your pet.

## CELEBRATE BY DOING SOMETHING YOUR PET LOVES

This can be a run on the beach or the dog park, a new bag of catnip or treats, or cleaning the fish's tank . . . do something loving as a gesture of appreciation.

## MARK THIS MILESTONE WITH QUIET TIME AND REFLECTION

It is lovely to mark a special milestone like this by remembering all the love and joy that has been part of being a pet parent. It is also helps reinforce the good in your relationship when you express thanks and gratitude.

Meditate on all the benefits you have derived from your relationship with your companion animal(s).

Write a love letter and share praise. Try making a list: *"I am grateful for my pet because . . . "* Even better, craft a love letter for your pet and read it to her/him. Even if your pet is fidgeting or seems not to hear, your love will radiate in your voice. Here's an example, short and sweet.

## SAMPLE LOVE LETTER TO MY PET

*Dear Jezabelle,*

*You are the sweetest and prettiest cat I have ever seen!*

*You came into my life when I was feeling low and sad, and you brought a great ray of hope and sunshine.*

*Your companionship has lifted me in so many ways, and I feel like I have returned to a state of joy and relaxation.*

*You are my confidante and friend,*

*My roommate and my playmate,*

*It is such security knowing you are there!*

*I love and appreciate you.*

# Chapter Six

*Commitment Ceremonies for and with Pets*

*"Before I would ever let my Italian Greyhound breed, I would give her a proper ceremony."*

—JANE STACEY

First of all, we want to offer this ceremony for animals that are serious about each other and have been sniffing at each other for a while . . . or those who deserve a blessing before they are brought together for mating purposes. Since marriage is a sacred event, you don't want to marry your dog or any other animal as a joke. (Okay, it can be fun, but be careful who you promise your pet's love or virtue to!) Use this Pet Commitment Ceremony for true soulmates and for animals destined to be brought together for breeding purposes.

Obviously, dogs tend to tie the knot more than other animals, but feel free to adapt this for any pet.

# Wedding Ceremony for Pets in Love

**HOW TO PREPARE:**

- Get bridal outfits or accessories for the animals (cute, but optional).
- Prepare a wedding altar by draping tulle or a white cloth over a table.
- Place a loving cup or special chalice filled with fresh water for the "bride and groom" on the altar.
- Bring a camera—you must take photos!

## GREETING

Welcome everyone. Puppy love gathers us here. Today, we celebrate the love between a couple that see each other as the Cat's Meow! Let us all offer our good wishes and blessings as they enter into sacred union.

## OPENING PRAYER

Let us begin by sharing a moment of prayer.

*Dear Creator of all life,*
*Look with favor upon the world you have made,*
*and especially upon these two dogs.*
*May this union be blessed in all ways and*
*May this duo and*
*all who have come to witness their union*
*be uplifted and embraced by love.*

## LOVING CUP CEREMONY

*(Hold the chalice filled with fresh water)*

We now take a special moment for these two to toast their love, devotion, and friendship. From the Celtic tradition, we use a "loving cup," from which these two will share their first sip/slurp as a married couple.

*To pets:* Today you become a part of each other in sacred kinship. Now, please drink to the love you share.

*Place cup on the floor. They slurp.*

## I DOS

Now, Fido, do you take Doris to be your beloved?
*Fido: Arf.*
And do you, Doris, take Fido to be your beloved?
*Doris: Arf.*

## FINAL BLESSING

*We bless these two in the name of friendship.*
*We bless these two in the name of playfulness.*
*We bless these two in the name of joy.*
*We bless these two in the name of fertility (if desired).*
*May they never hunger for dog biscuits and always be filled with love!*
*May this union be blessed in all ways.*

## PRONOUNCEMENT

As we have heard and witnessed your "arf" and desire to be united, we now pronounce you two pooches in love! Go ahead and lick the bride.

# Including Your Dog in Your Wedding

*"I plan to have my dog walk down the aisle with our rings around his neck. He's always at family events. Everyone expects him to be there. He goes wherever I go. He loves to be included in everything. So why not down the aisle?"*

—KATHLEEN VERA

**HOW TO PREPARE:**

- *Get a snazzy outfit for your pooch.*
- *Arrange for someone to be in charge of your pet so you don't have to be.*
- *Make sure your pet has an opportunity to go to the bathroom before walking down the aisle.*
- *Make plans for someone to hold the dog during the ceremony.*
- *Don't invite a dog to a wedding reception, unless he is very small or very well behaved and completely supervised.*

We've seen everything from a dog in a tutu, acting as the maid of honor, to tuxedo-clad dogs as ring- or vow-bearers. We've seen more than one overdressed dog come down the aisle or show up at a ceremony. One woman, a guest, brought a dog in her shoulder bag. Our dog trainer Anthony Jerone, of the Academy of Canine Training, shared that he had fifty dogs at his wedding. They had a minister who was an animal activist. It was a very dog-friendly celebration in Queens, New York. But don't try that at home—unless you have a big backyard (or a willing venue) and plenty of plastic bags.

## IDEAS FOR INCLUDING YOUR POOCH AT YOUR WEDDING

- Have someone walk him or her, and sit with the dog and bring a chew toy to keep him or her busy!
- Don't give the animal *real* rings to hold.
- Make sure the area is enclosed.
- Make sure there is a place to take the pooch if he or she gets bored, restless, cranky, or barky.
- For dogs, as well as cats, gerbils, birds, or dogs who cannot attend—mention them in the ceremony. (That goes for honoring deceased pets as well!)
- Include pets in your written wedding program with both photo and acknowledgment.
- Keep the pet's photo on your wedding altar or at the family photo table.
- Donate money to the ASPCA, the Humane Society, or favorite shelter in lieu of favors.

## DOGGIE VOWS

Here's a beautiful way Joe Jeydel and Kate Bartoldus-Jeydel worked their doggie into their wedding ceremony. Kate and Joe met on a warm Manhattan night when Joe's dog Duke insisted on a second nighttime stroll down familiar city streets, where they ran into Kate for the second time that evening! This is what they read to one another at their wedding:

**Joe:** *I stand here before you today, the most important and significant day of my life so far, because of a single soul, an unlikely soul at that—Duke. Not only is he the reason that you walked up to me the first time, but if it wasn't for his need to go out just two hours later, I would have missed you the second time around. He knew then, as I know now, that you were perfect. Perfect in so many ways. I let you go once, but I will never let you go again. I came to New York City because of my job, but the dreamer in me, no matter how concealed and quiet he might be, would tell you that I came here to meet you, and I cannot deny that. I love that and I love you.*

**Kate:** *For once and for all, you need to know that Duke was not the only reason we met that night. As I walked home and saw your incredible smile for the second time, something in me recognized you. Even though we had never met . . . something in my soul let me take the deepest, most peaceful breath of my life because in the middle of millions of people, I had found you . . .*

*That's not to say that everything is always perfect or as story-book as that first night, because to say that would take away from how rich and textured you've made my life.*

*I remember one night early on in our relationship, we had an argument about something or other, and I was sure that it would be the end of us. I was so upset, I just sat on the kitchen floor with my head in my hands. But then I looked up and saw you sitting right next to me. Without ego or pride, we sat there on that awful linoleum floor until we figured it all out. That is why I knew I'd marry you and I can promise you, come what may, that I will always sit on the kitchen floor until we figure it out. I love you with a bigger heart than I ever knew I had. You are my peace, my joy, and, thankfully, my family forever.*

# Pet Tale:

*Greeting the Day with Joy*

BY REVEREND VICTOR FUHRMAN

Our dog, Kismet, greets me every morning with unbridled enthusiasm and joy, wagging her tail like a white-and-maroon propeller, jumping up and holding on to railings so that she can be closer to me, and licking my face every chance she gets. In one of those "Aha" moments, it occurred to me that she is greeting the day with the innocence and joy of a child, appreciating all the gifts in her life, and thanking me, her "master," for those gifts in the only way she knows how.

It stirred my heart and soul, because it reminded me of a lesson learned and forgotten long ago, in a world where demands and pressures sometimes blur the memory. That lesson is from teachers and sages who tell us to give thanks, every day upon awakening, to "Our Master," the Divine Creator in whatever form we acknowledge this universal being: God, Goddess, or All That Is. I remembered how this simple act can completely change the energy of the day and quickly erase any negativity or ill feeling that we may have awakened with.

I realize that Kismet is saying to me, "Thank you for allowing me another day of life . . . another day of possibilities . . . another day to experience the full spectrum of life . . . another day to make choices. I am grateful for my life and, with your loving guidance, will do my best to live it with joy and love. Thank you!"

The relationship to our pets is deepened and enriched by sharing "real life." It's important to acknowledge and celebrate these moments. They are simple tributes and moving meditations that connect us with the animals we love. They are as important as any pet prayer ever spoken; they represent the bond between us and our pets.

## Part Three
## Summary Prayer

*Let us celebrate the days of our lives with our pets*
*And ask that life grants us the right circumstances*
*to make them*
*part of our holidays, family gatherings, and our every day.*
*We ask for support in making our celebrations joyous*
*and safe*
*for pets and their humans.*
*We ask that through our relationships with our*
*pets we learn more*
*about ourselves and our connection to all living things.*
*Let us dance with our pets. Sing to our pets.*
*Exercise with our pets. Swim with our pets.*
*Play like a kid with our pets. Watch TV with our pets.*
*Let us share life with our pets and*
*appreciate the life we share.*
*May our days with our pets be good and long on Earth.*

# Part Four

*Pet Prayers, Blessings, and Spiritual*
*Practice for Every Day*

"A workman in my home inadvertently left a door open
and my cat got out one day. I was devastated. I sat out on
my patio with her food dish in hand, shaking it and calling
to her all night long. Neighbors were having a loud party. I
feared my timid little cat would never walk past the noise
to come home. All of a sudden I felt there was nothing
more to do but pray, so I did. Turned out, she was
under my neighbor's car, keeping warm. My
grandson found her the next day. Did my
prayer work? I choose to believe it did."

—SUNNY LEE

# Chapter Seven

*Pet Prayers and Blessings for All Occasions*

Your pet has no religion, yet those of us who like to pray and live spiritually often include our pets in our prayers, spiritual experiences, and religious practices. We pray for their well-being and their health; we bless them in their daily life; and we pray for the patience, fortitude, and compassion to get through the challenging times. Here is a smattering of nondenominational and interfaith prayers and practices for daily life.

# Prayers Representing and Inspired by the World's Traditions

For pet owners who would like to honor their own faith or other traditions, these prayers are adapted from the world's religions.

## HINDU BLESSING TO REMOVE OBSTACLES

This evokes the Hindu God, who is famous for having the head of an elephant and known as the God who is worshiped first because he removes all obstacles to prayer.

*From the Hindu tradition,*
*we ask first for the blessings of Lord Ganesha,*
*Remover of Obstacles and bringer of success.*
*We call to him of the elephant head*
*for certainly he knows the animal spirit.*
*May he remove all obstacles to this pet's well-being.*
*May he support this animal in daily survival and needs for*
*all time.*
*May he pave the way for a good and happy life.*
*May he bring peace and ease to this creature, as we evoke him:*
*Om Ganesha. Om Ganesha. Om Ganesha.* (Repeat three times).

## THE PET'S PRAYER

*Divine Spirit of all living things,*
*In your name we pray.*
*Please guide us in the care of this animal.*
*Teach us how to be good pet parents.*
*Ensure that we learn the skills and abilities.*
*Allow us to call upon your sacred love*
*and your nutritious bounty*
*to feed our beloved pet.*
*Let us nourish his/her spirit as we provide daily bread.*
*Please bring the wisdom of the animal kingdom*
*into our home,*
*for we call upon the power and the glory*
*of your holy wisdom*
*to treat this loved one as a holy child of yours.*
*Amen.*

# CATHOLIC PRAYER FOR BLESSING
# OF THE ANIMALS

During the Feast day of St. Francis, churches around the world participate in the blessing of the animals. This blessing is by Father Paul Keenan, used with permission, from his book *Why We Love Them So* (Illumination Books, 2007).

*"Lord God, we bless and praise you for the wonders of your creation, for its rich variety and its immeasurable abundance.*

*"In your wisdom and love, you created the birds of the air, the fish of the sea, and every living creature and gave to us dominion over them.*

*"They enhance our lives in so many ways and by their very presence give glory to you. They rely on us, as they rely on you, for their well-being.*

*"And so, Father, we ask you to bless (name of animal) here present. May he/she be a living example of your watchful care, and may you grant him/her health, happiness, caring people, and everything needed for the joyous life you intend for him/her.*

*"Praise and glory be to you, Lord God, for ever and ever. Amen."*

—FATHER PAUL KEENAN

## CHRISTIAN PRAYER FOR PETS

Adapted from the Catholic blessing of the animals

*May (pet's name) be blessed.*
*May she fulfill her days on earth*
*and lead the life God meant for her.*

## MUSLIM BLESSING FOR ANIMALS

Adapted to honor the essence of Muslim belief. This is not directly from the Koran.

*In the name of Allah,*
*the beneficent, the merciful.*
*Praise be to the Lord of the*
*Universe who has created us and*
*all things.*
*Give us good animals and protect them.*
*You are the one who hears and knows all things.*
*Let our pets be your servants, as are we.*
*Most gracious are those who walk on*
*the earth in humility.*

## JEWISH PET PRAYER

*Lord, our God, who created heaven and earth,*
*and who led Noah to fill his ark with animals in pairs,*
*and who spared the animals so that they may live and*
*procreate on the earth again,*
*I pray that my pet walk the path of the Most High,*
*alongside me.*
*May he/she be uplifted in your holy love*
*and be kept safe beneath your watchful eye.*
*Let my pet feel secure, and never scared.*
*May my animal rest in you, safely and securely.*
*Please bless my beloved pet in all ways.*

## HEBREW BLESSING

*Blessed art thou, Lord our God, King of the Universe, who made*
*me to be a faithful companion to Adam and Eve and their*
*descendants.*

*Thank you for creating me and giving Adam the wisdom to*
*give me the Hebrew name, KeLev, which means "like the heart."*

*I pray to be true to my name. Arf-Mein!*

## BUDDHIST PRAYER

*Let us recognize all animals, for they are beings of our earth.*
*Let us give thanks for their presence,*
*for they bring love and joy to our lives.*
*May all animals be free from suffering,*
*and those things that cause it.*
*May all beings know the sacred happiness.*
*May we celebrate the equality of all that lives.*

## BLESSINGS OF THE GODDESS

*We pray to the Great Goddess, Mother of all things,*
*to take this sweet soul to her heart,*
*to nurture, feed, and help him grow.*

*We ask the Lady of the Beasts to welcome this furry little one*
*into the warmth of her circle of animal friends*
*that he may live a life rich with connection to his other furry kin.*

*We ask the Goddess to love and protect this child of hers.*
*May she uplift and embrace this furry soul.*
*And grant him a joyous life,*
*Filled with love, play, and plenty to eat.*
*And so it is!*

# NATIVE AMERICAN PRAYER

Great Spirit, please watch over
my dear friend, the four-legged one.
Her love for me is true.
She is protectress. Playmate. Sister.
She brings joy and peace.
She offers comfort and understanding.
She assures playtime and exercise.
Her heart is near and dear to mine.
Great Spirit, please care for her.
Protect her. Keep her healthy.
May her days be good and long on earth.

# Blessings for Daily Activities

You don't need a special celebration or a holiday to bless your pets or pray for their well-being. Here are some all-purpose prayers that can be used throughout the day to surround your pets with love and protection.

## WAKE-UP AND BEDTIME PRAYER

*May Divine Love bless you and keep you.*
*May Divine Love be gracious unto you.*
*May Divine Love give you now, and, forever, that most precious gift . . . Peace.*

## PRAYER OF PROTECTION

*May this pet be guided in her everyday activities.*
*May she be safe in her comings and goings.*
*May she be well-fed, well-manicured, and look both ways before crossing the street . . . or before crossing another animal.*
*May she be protected by the force of life that brought her to us.*
*May she be safe in our home.*
*May she be safe in our absence.*
*May she be safe in our presence.*
*May she be safe and guided every day.*

## MAY THE ARCHANGELS GUIDE YOUR PET

Adapted from a prayer we hear all the time at the New Synagogue, from Rabbi Joseph Gelberman and Rabbi Roger Ross. Rabbi Gelberman asks us to use this prayer with his blessings and says "it belongs to everyone."

*Please set the guiding light of Uriel before our pet to light his way.*
*Please set Michael to the right to aid and protect him.*
*Please set Gabriel to the left for clarity and to aid him in expressing his truth.*
*Please set Raphael behind him to keep/make him strong, healthy, and well.*
*And so it is.*

# A GUARDIAN ANGEL FOR YOUR PET

They say pets are our guardian angels, but who watches over them? You can ask the pets you have loved—and lost—to do the job.

*May this animal be blessed with special angels to watch over her.*
*May she be helped along by our beautiful angel pets on the other side.*
*May they be her guardians, keeping her safe and in balance.*
*May they whisper in her ear, in the language of light,*
*and guide her in anything she needs to know.*
*May they help her fulfill her purpose here on earth*
*and bless her life in all ways.*

# BLESSING OVER PET FOOD

*May this food be nutritious
and delicious.
May it be wholesome
and fulfilling.
May it help you enjoy
the blessings nature brings.
May it satisfy your hunger,
help you grow stronger,
make your coat shinier,
and ensure your good health.
May this food be blessed in all ways.*

# MOTHER EARTH FOOD BLESSING

*Mother Earth,*
*on behalf of our pet,*
*we thank you for the abundance*
*of your body*
*and for the offering of this meal.*
*We appreciate the goods and gifts you give naturally.*
*May they bring good nutrition,*
*strong bones, good teeth, and delight*
*to our sweet pet.*
*May this food be savory*
*and satisfying.*
*And so it is.*

## G'NITE PRAYER

(For any night, or on those nights when you finally get your
pet to bed!)

*Sleep, little loved one,*
*snug in your bed.*
*Let visions of your favorite things*
*flow through in your head.*
*Let go the day*
*so you can be refreshed overnight.*
*Tomorrow we'll start fresh*
*and we'll start the day right.*
*If I yelled or ignored you*
*or didn't pet you enough*
*forgive me, I will do better tomorrow,*
*because I love you so much!*

# Prayers for Special Pet Situations and Frustrating Moments

Pet parents know that just as toddlers and kids can be a lot to handle, puppies, kittens, and other animals sometimes get on your nerves or wear you down with their behavior. These prayers are a "Spiritual S.O.S" for those times when you feel you are at the end of your rope. When your pets are driving you crazy, sit quietly for a moment and say:

## NATIVE AMERICAN PEACE PRAYER

*Peace to my right.*
*Peace to my left.*
*Peace in front of me.*
*Peace in back of me.*
*Peace above me.*
*Peace below me.*
*Peace within me.*
*Peace all about.*
*Peace abounds.*
*Peace is mine.*

## PROTECTING YOUR HOUSE FROM A
## DESTRUCTIVE PUPPY

*When I leave the house for work,*
*please let me believe in my heart*
*that I will return to a normal house,*
*not a home destroyed and pulled apart.*

*Please guide my pet to be her best*
*and to not mess with all my stuff.*
*'Cause every time I go away*
*she ruins something . . . and I have had enough.*

*So if you can, and if you might,*
*please protect my home from her scratch and bite.*
*And let her outgrow the habit to destroy*
*the couch, the rug, and every toy.*

*I would like to come home to joy and peace,*
*to walk in the door and sigh relief.*
*Want to see that my stuff is all okay,*
*and that she has had a peaceful day!*

## PRAYER FOR PATIENCE

*Divine Spirit of all there is,*
*please fill me with your divine presence,*
*and your divine patience.*
*I need help dealing with my pet's*
(behavior problem, missing the litter box,
destructive ways, etc.)
*Please show me what I need to do to make things right.*
*Please bring balance back to my home.*
*For this I pray.*

## FOR TRAINING A DOG

*(Adapt for other animals)*

*God grant me the patience and faith to train this animal.*
*May I be loving, yet firm.*
*May I see, and rejoice in, small successes.*
*May I recognize and be open to new ways to approach my pet.*
*May I connect deeply with the soul of his/her being,*
*and be guided by her/his highest self.*
*May we together approach the training process from the highest*
*place of wisdom and love.*

## FOR PETS THAT MESS

*Please help me train my pet to "go" in the right place.*
*Give me the courage to stay on top of this process and to be*
*consistent.*
*Give me the patience to love my animal through this phase*
*and to stand firm in this training experience.*
*May I have the strength to persevere.*
*May my pet meet me halfway and come closer each day.*
*And when I have to bend down and clean it up off the floor,*
*may I still have faith that this is a temporary experience,*
*And that she will come out of it well-trained and well-behaved.*

## FOR HOUSE PETS THAT DO NOT GET ALONG

Inspired by the prayer of St. Francis

*Divine Ruler of all pets,*
*please fill our home with your sacred spirit*
*and bring balance to our animals.*
*Where there is fighting, may there be peace.*
*Where there is rejection, may there be acceptance.*
*Where there is frustration, may there be resolve.*
*Where there is dominance, may there be equality.*
*Where there is fear, may there be love.*

# FOR HEALING ALLERGIES

*Please, God,*
*heal my allergies to my pet (or my loved one's pet).*
*Heal my sinuses.*
*Fix my breathing.*
*End my congestion.*
*Soothe my irritated skin.*
*Stop my itchy nose from running.*
*Build my ability to tolerate allergens.*
*Show me how to heal myself*
*and help me rise above this challenge.*
*Direct me to the best medical care,*
*with the most helpful holistic complements.*
*And help me know the true root of this allergy.*
*Help me heal.*

## PRAYER FOR PEACE IN THE ANIMAL WORLD

*We pray to God to eradicate all the suffering in the animal world:*
*We pray that generosity triumph over indifference,*
*that compassion triumph over apathy,*
*that love triumph over despair.*

## PRAYER FOR ANIMALS IN SHELTERS

*Dear God,*
*Please bring the right owners*
*to the right pets,*
*at the right time.*
*Make matches that will*
*help these sweet ones in shelters*
*find good homes*
*and true families,*
*where they can love*
*and will be loved*
*and cared for*
*for all the days of their lives.*
*Amen.*

# BUDDHIST PRAYER
## FOR STRAY AND HOMELESS

We call upon Green Tara,
may she offer her protective presence
and her healing light.
To all the fur-beings who are lost,
or homeless,
or living as strays,
may they find a good meal to eat.
May they have shelter to keep them warm.
May they have comfort.
May they be shown kindness by strangers.
And may they, if they choose, find a good home.
May they rest in a place in which they can thrive.
Filled with love,
with warmth,
with tender caring,
with good food,
with true companions
for all of their days.

## PRAYER AND FENG SHUI PRAYER AND
## RITUAL FOR A LOST ANIMAL

Put a photo of your beloved pet in the near right corner of your home (this is near right, from where you walk in the door). In feng shui, that is the "helpful people" corner. Fill the pet's name in on the top line. Fold and place the prayer under the photo. Every day, at a time when the pet's feeding time would be, read this prayer aloud (with your children, if you have any, as their prayers are always heard first!).

*Divine Spirit of All There Is:*
*Our pet's name is _____*
*He is deeply loved and cherished in our home.*
*He is someplace where we cannot see him now.*
*Please keep him safe and warm.*
*Please make sure he has food and water.*
*Please give him shelter and protection.*
*Please reveal to us how we can find him.*
*Or lead him back to us by the miracle of your nature.*
*Our hearts, home, and arms remain open.*
*Please guide us to him and guide him back to us.*
*For this we pray.*

# Pet Tale:

## *The Special-Needs Poodle That Changed My Life*

BY HOLLY FAIRCHILD

I believe that all of our pets come to us for a reason and not by accident, the same way as the people in our lives are there for a reason. That's how I knew that the miniature chocolate poodle that showed up in my life was meant to be.

Up until then I had only had cats and decided to do research on dogs to ensure that I chose a good breed with a good temperament. This was not in my usual nature of "leap now and ask questions later," so I was very proud of myself for doing the responsible thing. I narrowed my preference down to a male miniature poodle that was brown in color, because they are not that common.

Then I began to search for such a dog and had no luck at all.

One day I saw an ad in the newspaper that someone was selling a litter of miniature poodles, so I called up and, sure enough, they had a male that was brown. As soon as I went to see the dog, though, I sensed that there was something wrong with him. He was small and didn't play with the other puppies, but instead just wandered off and cried because he seemed to be lost. Someone else had spoken for him but hadn't confirmed yet, so I didn't worry too much about whether or not to take him.

I had kind of written him off when, a week later, the owner called to say that the other person couldn't take him and he was still available. This time, my husband came with me, and by then there was only one female left, who looked very healthy... and this little guy whose sister didn't want anything to do with him! I could see that he still didn't seem right, and I suggested to my husband that maybe we should take the female instead, but my husband said, "No, you came for the male and you should take the male."

And there began a four-year journey of caring for Daunte Carter Moss (my husband is a Vikings fan), a dog that was partially blind, hard of hearing, and had brain damage and rage syndrome.

It took six months to convince our vet that he was having trouble seeing. Within four years, he had accumulated forty-four pages of medical records. Because of his brain damage, it was impossible to train him to do his business outside, even with private sessions with a professional dog trainer. However, after a year we did manage to train him to use puppy training pads. Soon our house had dog odors, and our friends and family stopped coming around because of the smell—plus they were afraid of getting bit. Our lives were consumed with caring for this severely disabled dog. Our vet described the degree of maintenance Daunte required as similar to caring for a child with Down syndrome.

He had to be carried up and down stairs because he couldn't see the steps, and it was almost impossible to find anyone willing to care for him when we went on vacation. At about a year and a half, his hip joints were weak to the point where my husband had to push him in a baby stroller to take him for a walk. And if this seems like a funny sight, try to imagine being a large Native Indian man pushing a poodle around the reservation in a baby stroller! Smart-alecky neighbors would call out, "Hey, Henry, what kind of dog is that?" and he would yell back, "It's a brown dog, okay?"

Looking back, I have no doubt that Daunte came into our lives for a very specific reason and we were chosen to be his caregivers. It was difficult understanding why all my hard work of preparing to own my first dog would be rewarded in such a way, but I knew somewhere along the way I had agreed to do it.

Daunte was still with us when I first saw my new dog, Echo. Daunte had to be put down a month after Echo came to live with us, when his health failed and nothing else could be done for him. My husband and I sincerely believe that Daunte chose Echo to be with us, to help us cope with his impending departure.

I have a little ornament of a chocolate poodle with a set of angel wings and a gold halo over its head that I think of as my little Daunte, now whole, and in heaven with his Creator.

# Part Four
# Summary Prayer

*Our relationships with our animal companions are sacred.*
*We ask that prayer,*
*blessings, and*
*and spiritual practice*
*be woven into our daily lives*
*and into the lives of our pets.*
*May each day with them be blessed.*
*Sacred.*
*Special.*
*And holy.*
*And so it is.*

# Part Five

*Healing for Pets (and Humans)*

"The fear and concern for a sick animal . . .

it's the worst kind of worry . . . "

—KATHRYN JANE

# Chapter Eight

*Prayers for When Your Beloved Pet Is Ill*

One of the most heartbreaking experiences for many of us is to find that our beloved animal companion has fallen ill. In many ways, it may be as trying and stressful as when illness strikes a spouse or child.

Cat lovers can relate to the unnerving experience of coming home from work and finding that instead of eagerly waiting for you at the door, your tabby is curled up on a chair with a listless look in his or her eyes, little energy, and a strained meow. Or finding that your dog is suffering with a sprained paw, resulting in a frightening limp. Fish and bird keepers know what it's like to see their precious companions taking refuge in a secluded part of their aquarium or cage while coping with low energy or an infection.

As with any illness or accident, human or animal, traditional medical care must come first. Prayer and other forms of spiritual healing are meant as complements to, not substitutes for, traditional Western medicine. Call your veterinarian and follow his/her instructions.

Once medical care is arranged, there are a wide variety of prayers and spiritual modalities available to assist you and your pet on the healing journey.

All of the following prayers are offered as guidelines, and we encourage you to adapt them to your personal spiritual practice and beliefs. If your pet is small enough and can be held without causing additional discomfort, we suggest holding the animal in your lap. For larger pets, gently placing your hand on them while praying creates a wonderful, loving connection.

# Healing Prayers

Every tradition has a way to call out to a divine spirit for healing and help in recovering from illness. The power of prayer is always available to help.

## PRAYERS FOR FULL RECOVERY FROM MINOR INJURIES AND ILLNESSES

### Nondenominational Christian

*Heavenly Father, please embrace our beloved (pet's name) with your divine compassion.*

*In your infinite wisdom and mercy, grant that (pet's name) be given the right medical care and treatment for this challenge.*

*We pray that if it be your will, (pet's name) enjoy a complete and full recovery, returning to his/her vibrant and joyous nature.*

*We thank you for the privilege of caring for this precious creature and we are grateful for your loving gift of healing. In Jesus' name, Amen.*

## SPIRITUAL JUDAISM

*Blessed art thou, Hashem, God and King of the Universe, who created all the animals as companions to humankind.*

*Grant that our companion, (pet's name), be returned to us healed and whole.*

*We pray that you send your healing angel, Rafael, to guide the hands and mind of the veterinarian caring for our beloved pet and that the recovery be swift with minimal discomfort.*

*We praise your loving kindness and limitless compassion. Amen.*

## INTERFAITH

*Father-Mother God, Great Spirit, we come to you with bowed heads, in humility and with open hearts, as we pray that you grant the boon of healing to our beloved (pet's name).*

*In your boundless wisdom, you brought (pet's name) into our lives.*

*We now pray for your mercy and compassion and ask that (pet's name) be restored to full health and vitality.*

*In gratitude for all of your gifts and blessings, we say Amen. And so it is!*

## BUDDHIST HEALING PRAYER

*We honor and acknowledge Kuan Yin,* Bodhisattva, *Goddess of limitless mercy, compassion, healing, and love.*

*Dear Goddess, please embrace our (pet's name) and use your healing unguents and essences to restore his/her health and spirit.*

*We thank you and praise you with the chant,* Om Mani Padme Hum, *"Hail the Jewel in the Lotus!"*

## PRAYER FOR OUR ANIMAL FRIENDS

This prayer is used with permission of The Pet Prayer Line, a prayer request Web site for sick pets and their human families at http://hometown.aol.com/prayersforpets/home.html.

*Heavenly Father, our human ties with our friends of other species are a wonderful and special gift from You. We now ask You to grant our special animal companions your Fatherly care and healing power to take away any suffering they have. Give us, their human friends, new understanding of our responsibilities to these creatures of yours.*

*They have trust in us as we have trust in You; we are on this earth together to give one another friendship, affection, and caring. Take our heartfelt prayers and fill Your ill or suffering animals with healing light and strength to overcome whatever weakness of body they have.*

(Here mention the names of the animals needing prayer.)

*Your goodness is turned upon every living thing and Your grace flows to all Your creatures. Grant to our special animal companions long and healthy lives. Give them good relationships; and if You see fit to take them from us, help us to understand that they are not gone from us, but only drawing closer to You. Grant our petitions through the intercession of good St. Francis of Assisi, who honored You through all Your creatures.*

—THE PET PRAYER LINE

# PRAYER FOR THE "HIGHEST GOOD"

When our special friends are seriously ill, we sometimes may not know how to pray for them. In our practice, we have adapted a prayer for the "Highest Good." When we pray for this, we are acknowledging that as human beings, we may desire a certain outcome; but what we desire may not be in accord with the divine plan. This type of prayer truly acknowledges that we relinquish our will to God's will with grace and acceptance.

*Spirit, we pray that you surround our companion (pet's name) with your mercy and love. We would love to see him/her healed and whole and ask this if it be your will.*

*We gracefully and gratefully accept your judgment and trust that the outcome be in accordance with your Divine Plan for the Highest Good.*

*Amen.*

# Pet Tale:

## *Saving Francis, the Drake*

BY MYSTL

The most meaningful experience I have had with a pet involved my drake Francis. I had him for eight years; he was teal in color, with iridescent blue and black feathers on his wings, just beautiful.

He had been attacked by the dog next door and was badly injured—and, of course, it was night, when the vet was not open. I brought him inside and made him as comfortable as I could in a box full of soft toweling. I prayed to Kuan Yin, Chinese Goddess of compassion, to help him not to suffer so much pain.

His whole back had been bitten and ripped. You could see the blood vessels. He was making a strange noise through his beak. I knew he was feeling pain. I had to do something to help him.

I must have gone into a trance or something, because I can't remember much. It was surreal, as if I were watching myself from outside my body, but I could see myself going through the motions of trying to heal him. There I was, going to the kitchen, opening cupboards, mixing and grinding something, going back to the laundry, back to the kitchen. It went on for ages. I remember putting something like a poultice on his back and saying one more prayer over him, and then going to bed.

The next morning, I rushed down the stairs to see if he had made it through the night . . . and he had! I dressed and took him to the vet. The vet could not believe me that it only had happened the night before. The scab that had formed looked like it was several days old. He asked me what I had used, but I could not remember. Whatever herbs and oils I had, I used.

The vet gave Francis an injection to stop any likely infection and a spray to keep flies and insects away from his back. When he was fully recovered, and all the feathers had grown back, you couldn't even tell it had ever happened! To celebrate his recovery, I got him a mate. The babies were so cute!

# Chapter Nine

*Healing Resources*

One of the blessings of our time is the Internet. There are many volunteer organizations that offer prayer and remote spiritual healing for both people and pets. Many neighborhoods have local prayer and spiritual healing groups that meet on a regular basis and also offer healing for pets. Check your local health food stores and holistic resource magazines for healing circles in your area. Reiki (an ancient form of hands-on healing) groups can be found in most cities, and many Reiki masters and practitioners, as well as other spiritual healing modalities, work with animals.

We believe that all of us have the capacity for spiritual healing, and the following simple techniques can be employed anywhere and anytime.

# Hands-On Healing

There are many healing modalities for animals, as well as human-based techniques that can be applied to your companion pets. Hands-on healing is one of the most natural, and anyone can do it.

**HOW TO PREPARE:**
- *Find a place where you and your pet can have some quiet, private time for at least fifteen minutes.*
- *The spot should be comfortable for both you and your pet, and allow you to either hold your pet or place it on a comfortable surface where you can easily reach all parts of the body without straining.*
- *Soothing music, gentle lighting, and nonirritating fragrance all enhance the experience for both healer and recipient.*
- *Wash your hands and dry them thoroughly before you begin.*

The practice of laying on of hands predates most Western religions and started with the shamans and medicine men and women of ancient cultures. At a minimum, laying on of hands is a physically and psychically comforting act. It extends the energy of love and compassion.

Most spiritual healing practices involving the laying on of hands work on the premise that we can tap the universal source of life energy and channel it through ourselves to others. In this way, we do not deplete our personal energy.

**BEGIN WITH A PRAYER OF YOUR CHOICE.** Ask for heavenly guidance and protection as you do this wonderful work.

**USE YOUR HANDS.** When you feel centered and ready, use your hands to "scan" your pet's body. Be aware of any subtle energies or feelings that you may sense. There is no right or wrong here . . . let your intuition guide you.

**FOLLOW YOUR INTUITION.** If you feel drawn to a specific area, gently place your hands there. If dealing with a wound or surgical site, make sure it is properly covered and apply only the lightest touch. (Note: It is not necessary to make physical contact for this to work. You can keep your hands a few inches away if you wish or if it makes your little beloved more comfortable.)

**LET THE ENERGY GUIDE YOU.** When you sense it is time to move your hands to another location, do so. Again, there is no right or wrong here, and those of us in practice believe that the energy is intelligent and goes where it needs to go.

**VISUALIZE A HAPPY OUTCOME.** When you feel comfortable with this process, you may want to close your eyes and use visualization to see your pet completely healed, happy, and playful. See the outcome as the current reality of now, rather than a goal yet to be obtained.

**EXPRESS GRATITUDE.** There will come a point when you sense that your session is complete (allow at least fifteen minutes). Use a closing prayer expressing gratitude for the gift of healing and the opportunity to use it.

**BRING THE HEALING SESSION TO A CLOSE.** Ask that the divine spirit close and protect your energy field and that of your pet. Take a few minutes to allow all of this to process; when finished, wash your hands once again. Drink lots of water and make sure your pet does also (if this is medically sound). These sessions may be repeated as often as you like.

# Prayer for Letting Go

There will come a point when veterinary and spiritual medicine have done all that they can. The hardest decision a pet owner will ever make is putting down a gravely sick or elderly animal. We strongly urge that if and when the time comes, you discuss this thoroughly with your vet.

After the quality-of-life and practical decisions have been made, prayer and meditation are effective tools for preparing to let our friends go. Here is a suggested prayer that may be used in the vet's office or prior to bringing your pet in.

## PRAYER FOR WHEN SAYING GOOD-BYE IS THE KINDEST DECISION

*Dear God, you entrusted me with the body and soul of (pet's name) for (number) years. During that time we grew together, played together, and enjoyed all of your bounties together. Now you call (pet's name)'s spirit back to you.*

*I pray that you take him/her gently, releasing the pain of the flesh and lightening the spirit as it rises to heaven.*

*I was grateful when you gave (pet's name) to me, and it is with gratitude that I return him/her to you. Amen.*

After praying, the vet may allow you to hold your pet as he or she gently departs. Take this opportunity to be present and bear witness to the transition. Project loving thoughts and visualize your pet's precious soul gently leaving the body and ascending to heaven.

Take some private time to grieve before leaving the vet's office and make sure you have someone there to support you on your return home.

# Prayers for Your Pets

You can now find cyber-prayer ministries online that are devoted to pets and their humans. If you want prayer support for your pets, these sites can be valuable.

**PET PRAYERS AND BLESSINGS INTERFAITH MINISTRY**
*Offers prayers, healing stories, and a blog.*
www.PetBless.com

**PRAYERS FOR PETS**
www.prayersforpets.org

**PET PRAYER LINE**
hometown.aol.com/prayersforpets/home.html

**GOD BLESS THE ANIMALS**
www.godblesstheanimals.com

**ANGELS AND MIRACLES PRAYER TEAM**
*Although they predominantly pray for humans, they are pet friendly.*
www.angelscribe.com

# Pet Tale:

## *A Furry Healer*

Sometimes it is our animals that heal us and
take us through life's transitions.

BY CAROLE MUMFORD

The hospital building looked tall and foreboding as I
approached in the darkness, but I knew this was one mission I
must accomplish. Dressed all in black, so as not to be noticed
by the guards, my friend and I came to execute a carefully
thought-out plan. Was this a devious terrorist plot? No, it was a
mission of mercy. In my arms huddled a furry bundle snuggly
wrapped in a baby blanket masquerading as my child. Normally
boisterous and loud, Max seemed to sense that this was a special job and he must remain quiet and still. This covert mission
involved "smuggling" my husband's furry "son" into the hospital room to bring my husband the comfort, love, and healing so
desperately needed. The hospital seemed unaware of the healing benefits such a visit could bring, so my friend and I
embarked on this as a covert mission.

I entered the building while my friend waited outside with our
"bundle" until I could unlock the back door from within.

Silently, we traversed myriad seemingly endless stairways leading up to my husband's floor. This might be the last time David would be able to pat Max's warm fur, so we were determined to succeed.

We made it past security and breathed a sigh of relief, we were in! Now, if we could just get past all the nurses and into David's room. Strolling nonchalantly, we closed our eyes and said a silent prayer that nothing would elicit a bark from my blanketed bundle. A nurse eyed us curiously, so I snuggled the blanket closer, rocking and cooing at my "baby," telling him what a good little boy he was. The nurse fell for the ruse, smiled, and went back to her duties. Whew, what a close call!

We had our goal in sight: my husband's room appeared at the end of a long hallway. We cautiously continued. Suddenly, a man walking close by gave us a strange look. I quickly glanced down at the blanket and saw that it had sprouted a tail! Was our cover blown? I hastily stuffed the tail under the confines of the blanket and breathed a sigh of relief when the man did a double-take as if he thought he must be seeing things.

We rushed the remaining way and opened the door to the hospital room. My friend stood as lookout at the door, and Max tumbled free, rushing to his "Daddy." He joyously leapt onto his bed, the two of them a blur of smiles and tail wags. As my husband hugged him happily, the torments of his long illness, the hospital, feeding tubes, shots, and medicine disappeared into a flurry of loving licks and happy little barks. For now, life had become normal again, as he was momentarily healed by the love of a furry companion.

During his illness, my husband was in and out of the hospital. I feel that the love, care, and compassion my dogs showed him every time he came home helped heal him and kept him feeling happy, calm, and loved. And, when he died, I would not have made it if not for the emotional healing I received from them.

# Part Five
## Summary Prayer

May God heal our animals,
and make them well and whole.
And may our animals
be allowed to continue to heal us.
Let us care for one another,
Companions. Friends. Family.
Let us travel the circle of life, together.

# Part Six

*Saying Good-Bye:*
*Remembrance Prayers and Memorials*
*When You Lose a Pet*

"And when I'm old and have slowed down,

I pray they understand,

and not look at me with a frown and dump me

in a strange new land.

But instead that they remember when we used

to run and play,

that they will love me to the end,

when I die and go away."

—LOREE (MASON) O'NEILL

© 2002 from *The Pet Lovers Prayer*

# Chapter Ten

*Prayers of Loss and Remembrance*

*"Planning and participating in a pet's funeral or
memorial service can bring great satisfaction to those who
mourn the loss of a cherished companion animal."*

—MARTY TOUSLEY

Losing a pet is like losing a family member. It is not less profound or less emotional than human loss. It is a death in the
family, and it comes with all the pain and grief that accom-
panies such an experience.

Some pet owners say it is *even more intense* because when
a beloved pet dies, we lose not only a cherished companion,
but a pure source of unconditional love. Acknowledging our
feelings of loss, and remembering our pets in a personally
meaningful way, ultimately helps us remember the love and
know that *it* never dies.

Creating a special grief ritual, such as a funeral, memorial, or private remembrance, helps with the grieving process and gives loved ones and family members a chance to support one another. It gives the grieving parties an opportunity for contemplation and reflection, as well as helping the natural grieving process begin its course.

You can opt to have a funeral a few days after the animal passes, or a have memorial months later, when you feel more ready to formally say good-bye. Perhaps some quiet time alone is all you need.

Private rituals, memorials, funeral services, and shared stories can all be healing, and can help you remain connected to your beloved pet in a healthy way. Pet owners can select from materials created for humans or create their own rituals and readings.

We hope you are aided and uplifted by these prayers, readings, and sample rituals and services.

# *Prayers to Ease the Pain*

Pet loss stirs pain. Pain is part of the grieving process. Acknowledging it brings us more powerfully to the other side of it. Allowing yourself to feel it and to mourn is essential.

## I MUST EMBRACE MY PAIN

*No one seeks out pain and sorrow,*
*but when it comes, we cannot just turn it away.*
*Loss is a part of life. Death is part of life.*
*Heartbreak is part of life.*
*We must accept it. We must embrace it.*
*We must embrace our pain,*
*As we once embraced our pets,*
*as if it were a good friend, a faithful companion,*
*for it brings a lesson to learn,*
*and it unfolds a strength we never knew.*
*If we are to live in the world, pain cannot be avoided.*
*Let us use pain, then, to grow and evolve.*
*Let us respect pain for its power to bring us to our knees,*
*and its ability to help us rise again.*
*Let us recognize pain for showing us how very much*
*alive we are.*
*And, by its contrast, for it is reminding us that we have*
*known joy.*

When we lose a beloved pet it is devastating at first.
Heartbreaking. Seems a loss too huge to bear.
But time heals all breaking hearts.
Good memories begin to gain strength over loss.
And once we pass through the worst, the darkest days,
we are stronger and better. We remember the best.
But what a great power there is in an open, hurting heart.
It is the sting of loss that eventually makes us stronger.
Then one day, there is a light at the end of the tunnel.
The sun seems brighter, and so does life.
We remember the one who has passed over,
but with a sense of blessing for all the love left behind.
A new day is born . . . and gratitude replaces sadness.

# THE RAINBOW BRIDGE

(This is considered a classic prayer for animals that have passed on. It is always identified as being written by "Anonymous.")

*Just this side of heaven is a place called Rainbow Bridge.*

*When an animal dies that has been especially close to someone here, that pet goes to Rainbow Bridge.*

*There are meadows and hills for all of our special friends so they can run and play together.*

*There is plenty of food, water, and sunshine, and our friends are warm and comfortable.*

*All the animals who had been ill and old are restored to health and vigor; those who were hurt or maimed are made whole and strong again, just as we remember them in our dreams of days and times gone by.*

*The animals are happy and content, except for one small thing: they each miss someone very special to them who had to be left behind.*

*They all run and play together, but the day comes when one suddenly stops and looks into the distance. His bright eyes are intent; his eager body quivers. Suddenly he begins to run from the group, flying over the green grass, his legs carrying him faster and faster.*

*You have been spotted, and when you and your special friend finally meet, you cling together in joyous reunion, never to be parted again. The happy kisses rain upon your face; your hands again caress the beloved head, and you look once more into the trusting eyes of your pet, so long gone from your life but never absent from your heart.*

*Then you cross Rainbow Bridge together.*

# Prayers for a Memorial or Remembrance Ritual

## I AM NOT GONE

*Do not stand at my grave and weep.*
*I am not there. I do not sleep.*
*I am a thousand winds that blow.*
*I am the diamond on the snow.*
*I am the sunlight-ripened grain.*
*I am the gentle autumn rain.*
*When you wake in the morning hush,*
*I am the swift, uplifting rush . . .*
*of quiet birds in circling flight.*
*I am the soft starlight, at night.*
*So do not stand at my grave and cry.*
*I am not there. I did not die.*

—ANONYMOUS

## PSALM 23

*The Lord is my shepherd; I shall not want.*

*He maketh me to lie down in green pastures:*

*He leadeth me beside the still waters.*

*He restoreth my soul.*

*He leadeth me in the paths of righteousness for his name's sake.*

*Yea, though I walk through the valley of the shadow of death,*

*I will fear no evil: for thou art with me;*

*thy rod and thy staff they comfort me.*

*Thou preparest a table before me in the presence of*

*mine enemies:*

*Thou anointest my head with oil;*

*My cup runneth over.*

*Surely, goodness and mercy shall follow me all the days*

*of my life:*

*And I will dwell in the house of the Lord for ever. Amen.*

## INVOCATION/OPENING PRAYER FOR
## PET MEMORIAL

*Mother, Father, God, Divine Spirit of all that is, we ask to feel the grace of your presence with us today. Please surround us in a circle of your divine light. Please lift our hearts and souls with your divine love.*

*From all directions—south, west, north, east, above, below, and within—please be with us and guide us toward greater healing and acceptance of the loss of one so loved.*

*We ask for comfort and strength from the highest planes as we pay tribute to this beloved pet (name), who walked the earth with love in his/her heart.*

*Be with us, now, Great Spirit of all there is, as we remember one who is so close to you now. Let this circle be our sacred container in which to remember. And help our hearts know what our minds cannot fully understand—that death is but a gateway back into the circle of greater love. So be it, and so it is.*

# Remembrance Services

Just as we have funeral, memorial, and remembrance services for the humans we love, out beloved pets deserve the same. There are many ways to go about this. Here are several nonreligious ways to say good-bye.

## A PRIVATE GOOD-BYE RITUAL

**HOW TO PREPARE:**
- *Take some time out from your busy schedule.*
- *Set aside a half hour or more.*
- *Find a quiet, comfortable place to sit.*
- *Play a piece of music that opens your heart.*

While this time of loss is sad and painful, it helps to take a moment in silence to reflect on the memories of your beloved pet.

**TAKE A MOMENT.** Sit in a place where you will be undisturbed for a while, and make it a sacred moment.

**REFLECT.** Consider what a privilege it has been to have shared your life with such a special soul. Consider that each of our pets is assigned to us for a particular reason . . . and for a specific length of time.

**RECALL THE LESSONS AND THE LOVE.** As you hold your pet's memory in your heart, reflect upon how he/she came into your life and what you learned from him/her.

**KNOW THAT YOU ARE RICHER.** Focus on this until you rise above the tears, and you will become aware of a wealth of experiences that made your life richer in so many ways.

**CELEBRATE A LIFE.** Take joy in these memories and let them lighten your heart.

# Pet Funeral Service

Each of us has his/her own way of grieving and processing loss. All are equally valid and necessary for personal healing. The pet funeral service offers a unique opportunity to actively participate in closure and healing very soon after the animal's passing. The following service can be adopted as an actual graveside service or for use at a scattering of ashes. This service is offered as a guideline, and we invite you to use it to create your own personal ritual.

**HOW TO PREPARE:**

- *Mourners assemble at the appointed place.*
- *Each mourner is offered a white carnation to use during the closing of the ceremony.*
- *The acting officiant (owner, friend, or clergy) asks the mourners to gather around the designated area and begins.*
- *For a burial, provide a shovel so the mourners can help shovel earth into the grave.*
- *Decide beforehand if you plan to scatter pet ashes, if you are not having a burial.*

## OPENING REMARKS

Dear Ones, we are called here today to bid farewell to our beloved companion, (pet's name). As we prepare to return his/her remains to the earth, we open our hearts in gratitude and thanksgiving for the privilege of having had (pet's name) to care for.

Let us pray . . . Lord (*God, Goddess, Divine Spirit*), in your wisdom, kindness, and generosity, you have given us the gift of animal companionship and stewardship. Thank you for our time with (pet's name) and for creating his/her unique and special soul. We pray that you welcome (pet's name)'s soul back into your loving arms and keep (pet's name) until our time comes and we are reunited.

Please lighten (owner's name)'s heart and fill it with joyous memories as the grieving dissipates. And help us all to remember (pet's name)'s endearing qualities. Lord hear our prayer. Amen.

## GIVE MOURNERS THE OPPORTUNITY TO SHARE

At this time, we ask those of you who would like to share some of your happy memories of (pet's name) to reminisce with us.

## MEMORIAL READING

After the sharing, a reading such as "Rainbow Bridge" may be inserted here.

## INTERMENT OF THE PET

After the reading, the interment or scattering ashes may take place:

We now commit the earthly remains of (pet's name) to the earth from which it came. As we do this, we know (pet's name)'s soul is free and frolicking in God's heavenly meadow. (Remains lowered into grave.)

## FLOWER BLESSING

We now invite you to bless (pet's name)'s spirit by placing your loving thoughts and wishes into the flowers you are holding and one by one casting the flowers into the grave.

## SYMBOLIC OFFERING OF EARTH

After the flower ceremony and interment, the owner and anyone else may take the opportunity to place a shovelful of dirt into the grave. This is a very difficult act and is certainly not mandatory. Participants should discuss this during the planning of the service so that there is no awkwardness when the time comes.

## ALTERNATIVE—SCATTERING OF ASHES

We now release the earthly remains of (pet's name) to the earth from which they came. (Ashes are either released into the wind or dropped into a body of water nearby.)

## CLOSING OF SERVICE

(Owner's name) would like to thank you all for joining us here today to bid farewell to little (pet's name). (Any announcements can be inserted here, such as an invitation to a tea or brunch, if desired.)

Let us close with the 23rd Psalm:

### PSALM 23

*The Lord is my shepherd; I shall not want.*
*He maketh me to lie down in green pastures:*
*He leadeth me beside the still waters.*
*He restoreth my soul.*
*He leadeth me in the paths of righteousness for his name's sake.*
*Yea, though I walk through the valley of the shadow of death,*
*I will fear no evil: for thou art with me;*
*thy rod and thy staff they comfort me.*
*Thou preparest a table before me in the presence of*
*mine enemies:*
*Thou anointest my head with oil;*
*My cup runneth over.*

*Surely, goodness and mercy shall follow me all the days*
*of my life:*
*And I will dwell in the house of the Lord for ever. Amen.*

*Amen. Go in peace.*

# Memorial/Good-Bye Service

A memorial service can be conducted any time after the passing of a pet and does not have the same urgency as a funeral. A memorial implies that there is no body, or ashes, but you can certainly decide to conduct a memorial service with the animal's ashes present, and you can also choose to scatter the ashes on the day of the memorial. This example service was crafted for a cat named Billy.

## INVOCATION/OPENING PRAYER

*Let us pray . . . Dear God, Divine Spirit of love and compassion,*
*grace us with the light of your presence with us today.*
*Surround us in your love, as we gather in this time of sorrow.*
*Uphold us as we offer a heartfelt tribute to Billy,*
*and as we seek to comfort the heartbroken humans who have*
*loved and adored her.*

*Dearest Creator, we pray,*
*gently guide the soul of this beloved furry baby, back*
*home, to you.*
*Hold her close. Renew her. Embrace her in your divine arms.*
*Let her run free and be at peace.*

*And for those who grieve,*
*please bring the gentle knowing that she is in a beautiful place.*
*That she is safe, that she is whole, that she is healed.*
*That her spirit lives on.*

*And to Billy wherever you may be.*
*Run free now, leap from the physical body that constrained you.*
*You are blessed.*
*There is no pain now . . . only play.*
*Go to the ancestors who await you.*

*We thank you for all you have given us here, on Earth.*
*Know that you will be missed dearly*
*and remembered well.*
*We love you. Amen.*

## INSPIRATIONAL MESSAGE

Billy is now in a wonderful place that God created especially for our feline friends . . . Kitty Heaven.

Kitty Heaven is covered with the most plush carpet and catnip, where Billy can nuzzle and roll around all day long. There are lots of big comfy couches and overstuffed chairs for her to curl up on. And there's no need to worry about stretching her claws or digging them into the upholstery, because all of the furniture is self-mending and renews itself every day!

There are lots of mice running around Kitty Heaven to catch and play with . . . and in Kitty Heaven the mice are never hurt and actually enjoy being chased and caught and played with!

Kitty Heaven features Manna Cat Food! All that Billy has to do is think of her favorite flavors, and the Manna Cat Food tastes like the yummiest, best she's ever eaten. And, oh, yes, when it rains in Kitty Heaven, it doesn't rain water. It rains sweet cream and ice cream!

In Kitty Heaven, the angels know exactly how each cat loves to be scratched and stroked . . . and Billy is so content and happy with this extra special treatment.

God made Kitty Heaven for the cats we love . . . and everything there is absolute purr-fection!

## PARTING PRAYER

*Divine Spirit of all living beings,*
*please call St. Francis*
*to come escort this beloved companion*
*across the Rainbow Bridge.*

*Assign her to a place of honor,*
*for she has been a faithful and beloved pet.*

*Bless the hands that sent her to you,*

*for they did so in love and compassion,*

*freeing her from pain and suffering.*

*We thank you for the gift of her companionship here on Earth for (number) years.*

*We ask that her earth parents can feel comfort and strength from the highest planes as they adjust to their loss.*

*To Billy, we say move beyond this life,*

*flowing like water, free and formless.*

*Enter the arms of the Great Spirit, fearless.*

*Return to source of your being, the great source of love.*

*Rest your soul, heal, be young again.*

*Be blessed. Amen.*

# Pet Tale:

## *Remembering Katie*

BY DIANE BRACKETT

The day came when I knew that I had to do a last service for my old dog, Katie, a golden retriever/Irish setter. She could no longer walk with her back legs, and she had congestive heart failure. So, I made the appointment at the vet's office.

During her last night on Earth, I talked to her, told her stories about things we had done together throughout her life. I reminded her of how she had loved to swim and fetch sticks in the water, how she always tried to rescue me when I was swimming, how she loved to do feints with any ball, all the many memories . . . I lay beside her and we slept together one last time.

After she died the next morning, I took her body back to the house where she had lived as a young dog, and buried her there in the apple orchard under a tree. I thanked her spirit for sharing her life with me and prayed for my deceased relatives to greet her in the Light. It was one of the most profound experiences in my life.

I couldn't stop crying. I was devastated to lose Katie, the first dog that I had as an adult. Tears continued to stream down my face as I drove. Somehow I managed to drive back to where I was living and where Katie had spent her last months. I went outside to the backyard, sat down on the door stoop which overlooked our small backyard at the condo, and sobbed.

Then, through my tears, I saw a golden retriever/Irish setter puppy gambol toward me across the grass . . . and then it was gone. I *knew* as surely as I am sitting here typing that Katie had come to comfort me and tell me that she was happy to be free of her old sick body and that her spirit was rejoicing.

With that final gift from Katie, I was able to stop weeping, at last.

## Part Six
## Summary Prayer

Let us visit the depths of grief
and resurface, remembering the love.
And let us say a proper good-bye
to the animals we adore
and appreciate all that we shared.
Let us remember, they never truly leave us . . .
they have simply shed their form
and returned to grow younger
in the arms of our Divine Pet Parents.

# Part Seven

## Finding Your New Love: Drawing Your New Pet to You

"Not only is there always another good animal in need of a good home, but we must remember to be thankful for the time and love our animals give us while they are here."

—KENT C. GREENOUGH

# Chapter Eleven

*How Soon Is Too Soon to Get Another Pet?*

"I was devastated when my cat went missing, but one day, the thick clouds of grief seemed to clear. I looked up, and there was this kitten that looked just like the cat I'd lost. I wasn't ready to take her home, but every day I went to feed her in the grass at the local hospital. She took my mind off my grief. Then, one day I went and she was no longer there. I was okay about it because I realize it was Jessie telling me it was okay to move on. I think she may have been an angel disguised as a cat."

—CHARLOTTE BELL

# When Grief Gives Way to New Love

I remember the day our two goldfish died. They were Alexander's first pets in our new house, and I, Laurie Sue, had single-handedly kept them alive for three years—an outstanding accomplishment in itself! I got so used to seeing those little fish faces swimming to the surface to say *hi!* . . . okay, to get food. Still, they were like family. They lived so long, I never thought they would go. The day I walked into Alexander's room and saw one of them on its side, barely breathing, I was devastated. I got a straw and blew bubbles into their tank, hoping it would be like mouth-to-mouth resuscitation.

Frantic, I called my nephew the animal expert—he had given the fish to us—for advice. He told me once they start floating on their sides, they are close to the end. I couldn't believe it. I went online, seeking a miracle cure to stop a goldfish from dying. Every time I looked into the tank and saw our sweet pet struggling for breath, tipping over more and more to its side, I prayed that he would right himself. But it was futile. I was shocked at how unwilling I was to let him die. And then, when I realized how much he was suffering, I sat and kept a vigil with him, telling him it was okay to let go. When he finally took his last breath, it became clear that his tank mate was close behind.

I couldn't imagine that the second fish would want to stay there alone. They'd been together from the start.

When the first one passed, I took him into the yard in a brand-new Tupperware container and held a wake (attended only by me and a few bugs). I didn't want to bury him, because I knew the other one was close behind and wanted them to be together.

Within two days, both our fish were dead. I was amazed at the tears I shed.

On a Friday morning, after the family had gone to work and school, I grabbed my clergy stole, and took an old spoon, a pair of latex surgical gloves, and the stiff little fish bodies and dug a deep hole in the earth near an old tree. Something told me to dig deep, deep, deep. I remember thinking, why am I using a spoon and not a shovel? But I just kept spooning my way about two feet under. I lay them into their grave and prayed. And I cried. I cried and prayed, so loud, that I must have looked like a crazy woman out in the backyard.

The grief was so intense. It brought forth all the grief I had ever felt. They were just goldfish, but to me they were family. All weekend I felt the sadness over me like a pall. The tears and sorrow would grab me anytime. Even though we'd been looking for a doggie for Alexander, I was in no mood to look at other animals. Yet, somehow we ended up at a shelter and within moments, Kismet Brockway Fuhrman walked—

and licked—her way into our lives and by that night, into our home.

No one was more shocked than I that the dog we were meant to have would show up just two days after (so tearfully) burying our fish. I was awed at how I knew to dig the hole so deep, so that no animal could get to them in the backyard. Even though it seemed "too soon" to get another pet, my intuition was moving me in another direction. I have no doubt that we were supposed to meet Kismet on that day. I think I grieved so hard for my fish because my soul was cramming three to six months of grieving into forty-eight hours.

There is a belief held by many that we must grieve for a long time in order to move on. But it may not be true for everyone. Some people are capable of loving and caring for a new pet almost immediately. I was surprised to find that I was one of them. The grief was soon absorbed into the amazing amount of effort, dedication, and work it took to train and care for a puppy.

"Many people worry that getting another pet too soon after losing the one they loved so much is an act of disloyalty to the one who died—but like everything else in grief, that is a very individual matter and varies widely from one person to the next," says grief counselor Marty Tousley. She points out that there are some people who simply have enough love to go around. Some people need a longer time to grieve and heal, and that should be honored as well. "Then there are some people who discover that it's not so much that they go looking for another animal, but another animal just seems to find them," she says.

When the time is right for you, you'll know.

# Calling to the Cosmos for Your New Puppy (or Pet) Love

## WISH UPON A STAR RITUAL

When you are ready for a new animal to love, try this ritual.

**HOW TO PREPARE:**
- *On a beautiful night, go out in the fresh air and find your first star of the evening.*
- *As you gaze upon it, free your breath and release old energies as you welcome the new.*

## BREATHE IN NEW POSSIBILITIES

Breathe out sadness . . . breathe in joy.

Breathe out inertia and exhaustion . . . breathe in energy and vitality.

Breathe out feeling lost . . . breathe in new possibilities.

Breathe out feeling stuck . . . breathe in a breath of fresh air.

Continue to breathe in good energy and relax into it.

## NAME YOUR SPECIAL STAR

When you are ready:

Name your star after the animal you hope to have in your life. Make a wish upon the star and ask your companion animal to find his or her way home to you soon.

## PRAYER FOR THE RIGHT PET

This ritual will gently set your intention and begin to let the universe know you are ready for a new pet companion. Add this prayer to give power to your wish.

*Star light, star bright,*
*I wish upon you tonight.*
*I am ready now for my perfect pet,*
*let him/her be balanced, happy and strong,*
*with a good soul and endless capacity for love.*
*May our life be happy and sweet.*
*Just can't wait until we meet.*

# Visualization for a New Pet

The best place to meditate on finding a new pet is outside in nature. Travel a few feet into the garden or backyard, a short distance to a neighborhood park or nature preserve, or many miles to a favorite natural sanctuary. Wherever you go, pick a place in which you feel serene and secure . . . where you feel "at home."

**HOW TO PREPARE:**

- *Begin by finding a comfortable place to sit with few distractions, preferably in the shade.*
- *If possible, sit with your back against a tree, allowing your spine to feel the energy of the tree; its strength, endurance, steadfastness through all types of weather, and its natural cycle of seasonal change.*
- *Take the time to also ground yourself to the earth, visualizing that the base of your spine is rooted to the earth just like the tree.*
- *Have a notebook handy.*

# Meditation to Connect with Your New Pet

Begin by taking a series of deep cleansing breaths and prepare for the meditation. Allow all stress and strain to leave your body, and focus on being in the present moment. Close your eyes and allow your breath to return to its normal rhythmic pattern. Allow yourself to go deeper into relaxation and begin to visualize a small figure off in the distance.

Slowly watch it approach as its form takes on clearer shape and definition. Begin to notice the coloring . . . is it uniform or multishaded? Begin to sense the eyes. What color are they, and what are they saying to you? When your new pet comes close enough to touch, gently feel it and remember the sensations.

Watch this adorable creature play for you, and observe its personality. Finally, ask it its name and where you may find it. Listen carefully and remember what it tells you.

Having experienced meeting your pet, begin to make your journey back to the present place and time, remembering your observations and expressing gratitude for the opportunity to "meet" your new pet. When you are ready, take three deep cleansing breaths and open your eyes.

Reach for your notebook and journal the experience.

# POEM FOR A NEW LOVE

*New companion, come to me,*
*By grace of air or land or sea.*

*Share with me a new direction,*
*Filled with love and true affection.*

*My home will be yours, comfy and warm,*
*To nurture and shelter you from the storm.*

*With lots of toys and wholesome treats,*
*Our days will be filled with hours so sweet.*

*I will learn your language as you will mine,*
*We'll talk with squeaks or purrs, barks or signs.*

*My soul is ready and my heart is free,*
*New companion, please come to me.*

—VICTOR FUHRMAN

# Pet Tale:

## *The Cat that Came in from the Cold and Warmed My Grandmother's Heart*

BY MIKE DIAMOND

I have a history of taking in kittens and finding homes for them. But I never realized just how tuned in I am to their feline universes.

My grandmother's beloved cat died last fall. My grandmother was heartbroken but swore she would not get another cat, or any other animal for that matter. She threatened me, my mother, and my aunts about not showing up with any kittens. None of us did—physically, anyway.

For the following week, I had dreams about cats. One night, I dreamed that I was feeding stray cats on the patio in back of my grandmother's house. The next morning, I woke up, and there was a black cat out on the patio, so I gave her some cat food. Suddenly the dream came back to me, and I knew that this cat was going to be my grandmother's next pet.

Sure enough, within days of my dream, three of the women in the neighborhood, friends of my grandmother, approached her about the sweet black cat that had showed up on the patio.

Turned out everyone loved her, and took care of her, but they all had cats and could not take her in. At a very young age, she had already delivered three kitten litters, right near neighbors' homes. The women wanted to chip in to have her spayed so she wouldn't have to keep going through the cycle of homelessness and of giving birth on the streets. The problem was, it was winter and they didn't want to spay her and send her into the cold.

They asked my grandmother if she would be willing to take the cat in "temporarily" until she recuperated from surgery. That was a year ago.

Squeaky lives at my grandmother's now, and she is fat and happy. My grandmother adores her.

So my dream was a premonition of some sort. And as it worked out, it was a clever way for the universe—and three neighbors—to bring my grandmother a new animal companion.

# Part Seven
# Parting Prayer

Pets will come and pets will go
but their love will surely live on.
May it always warm your heart to know
they are still with you even when they've gone.
You have been dearly blessed
by the animals you have loved.
And they have been blessed by you!

# SPECIAL PRAYER PERMISSIONS

Part Four, page 100:

"Catholic Prayer for Blessing of the Animals," by Father
Paul Keenan, used with permission, from his book *Why We
Love Them So* (Illumination Books, 2007).


Part Five, pages 131–132:

"Prayer for Our Animal Friends," used with permission of
The Pet Prayer Line, a prayer request Web site for sick pets
and their human families at
http://hometown.aol.com/prayersforpets/home.html


Part Six page 149:

Quote from *The Pet Lovers Prayer*, used with
permission of Loree (Mason) O'Neill, © 2002

# INDEX

# ABOUT THE AUTHORS

**REVEREND LAURIE SUE BROCKWAY** has seen many pets walk down the aisle. She is a leading interfaith and non-denominational wedding officiant who specializes in creating highly personalized ceremonies for couples of all backgrounds and faiths. She is an expert on unique ceremonies and has a busy wedding ministry in New York (www.WeddingGoddess.com) and she is editor of Wedlok.com. She is the author of many books, including *Wedding Goddess: A Divine Guide to Transforming Wedding Stress into Wedding Bliss* and *The Goddess Pages: A Divine Guide to Finding Love and Happiness.*

**REVEREND VIC FUHRMAN, M.S.C., R.M.,** has always had a special relationship to animals and the ability to commune with them. He is an interfaith minister, spirituality teacher, healer, Reiki master, and writer who specializes in helping people (as well as pets) heal, transform, and enhance their lives. With his rich, soulful voice and broadcasting background, he creates meditations for healing, empowerment, and relaxation for Beliefnet.com and other organizations. He is the creator of www.EnerVision.org, a curriculum designed to teach psychic self-empowerment and healing.

Reverend Laurie Sue and Reverend Vic are a married couple who serve the world community individually and as a team. They are experienced interfaith ministers who are called to offer blessings of all kinds and have had the honor of presiding over many pet blessing ceremonies. They have been writing, creating, and delivering spiritual services for many years, individually and collaboratively. They worked together as chaplains for the Red Cross during recovery from 9/11. They are co-hosts of *Interfaith Living*, on www.qtworldradio.net. They live in New York with their teenage son, Alexander, and his best friend, Kismet.

Visit the Pet Prayers and Blessings Interfaith Ministry at www.PetBless.com.